WILLIAMS - SONOMA
BASICS COLLECTION

HEALTHY
FIRST
COURSES

WILLIAMS-SONOMA
BASICS COLLECTION

HEALTHY
FIRST
COURSES

GENERAL EDITOR
CHUCK WILLIAMS

RECIPES BY
DIANE ROSSEN WORTHINGTON

PHOTOGRAPHY BY
ALLAN ROSENBERG & ALLEN V. LOTT

WELDON OWEN

WILLIAMS-SONOMA
Founder: Chuck Williams

WELDON OWEN INC.
President: John Owen
Publisher/Vice-President: Wendely Harvey
Associate Publisher: Tori Ritchie
Project Coordinator: Jill Fox
Consulting Editor: Norman Kolpas
Recipe Analysis & Nutritional Consultation:
    Hill Nutrition Associates Inc.
    Lynne S. Hill, MS, RD; William A. Hill, MS, RD
Copy Editor: Sharon Silva
Art Director: John Bull
Designer: Patty Hill
Production Director: Stephanie Sherman
Production Editor: Janique Gascoigne
Co-Editions Director: Derek Barton
Co-Editions Production Manager (US):
    Tarji Mickelson
Food & Prop Stylist: Heidi Gintner
Associate Food & Prop Stylist:
    Danielle Di Salvo
Assistant Food Stylist: Nette Scott
Props courtesy: Sandra Griswold
Indexer: ALTA Indexing Service
Proofreaders: Ken DellaPenta, Desne Border
Illustrator: Diana Reiss-Koncar
Special Thanks: James Obata, Jennifer Hauser,
    Gina Louise Sciarra, Claire Sanchez,
    Marguerite Ozburn, Jennifer Mullins,
    Peggy Fallon, Mick Bagnato

The Williams-Sonoma Basics Collection
conceived and produced by Weldon Owen Inc.
814 Montgomery Street, San Francisco, CA 94133

In collaboration with Williams-Sonoma
100 North Point, San Francisco, CA 94133

Production by Mandarin Offset, Hong Kong
Printed in China

*Cover: Three-Lettuce & Walnut Salad (recipe on
page 83) can be put together in just a few moments,
although its rich taste belies its easy preparation.
Back Cover: Hearty Bean, Pasta & Zucchini Soup
(recipe on page 48) provides balanced protein and
plenty of dietary fiber along with good flavor.*

A Weldon Owen Production

Copyright © 1995 Weldon Owen Inc.
Reprinted in 1995

Library of Congress
Cataloging-in-Publication Data:

Worthington, Diane Rossen.
    First courses / general editor, Chuck Williams ;
recipes, Diane Rossen Worthington ; photography,
Allan Rosenberg & Allen Lott.
        p.   cm. — (Williams-Sonoma basics collection)
    Includes index.
    ISBN 1-875137-16-5
    1. Soups.   2. Salads.   3. Appetizers.
    I. Williams, Chuck.   II. Title.   III. Series.
TX757.W67   1995
641.8'1—dc20   94-25877
                                                    CIP

HEALTHY
FIRST
COURSES

CONTENTS

THE BASICS

The goal of a healthy first course is to begin a meal with good taste and style at the same time maintaining a balanced diet. While not a weight-loss guide, this book offers plenty of information and inspiration for eating wisely. A consensus of experts consider a healthy diet one in which 30 percent or fewer calories come from fat, about 15 percent from protein and about 55 percent from complex carbohydrates and one that is high in fiber and low in cholesterol and added salt. More than that, a healthy diet is one that uses a variety of fresh, seasonal foods combined in interesting, creative ways. To achieve a well-balanced diet overall, plan meals ahead, pairing a rich first course with a lean main dish one day and a healthy first course and a wicked dessert another. This chapter—like a good first course—sets the stage for what follows, offering guidelines for choosing and storing the nutritious ingredients used in the appetizer, soup and salad recipes that make up *Healthy First Courses.*

COOKING HEALTHY FIRST COURSES

It is ironic that the first course usually isn't the primary decision a cook makes when planning a menu. The main dish more likely comes first and then an appropriate recipe is chosen to come before it.

But first courses should never be an afterthought when planning a nutritionally balanced diet—one widely varied in nutrients, with adequate protein, high in complex carbohydrates and lower in fat and cholesterol. Literally, they help provide balance to a menu. For example, if a main course is generous in animal protein, an appetizer can be chosen for its carbohydrate content or to lower the overall percentage of calories the menu derives from fat. Conversely, if beans, grains or pasta will be the centerpiece of the meal, the first course might offer just a taste of poultry or seafood.

Obviously, such decisions become a question as much of aesthetics as of nutrition: A thoughtfully planned menu offers a variety of foods that progress logically and pleasingly from beginning to end. The first course recipes in this book aim to give you the widest possible variety of choices with which to begin a meal in style and good health.

MAKING A LITTLE GO A LONG WAY

Many classic appetizer ingredients have been dropped by the wayside as home cooks pursue healthier ways of eating. But if used sparingly, the following rich, flavorful foods can enhance all kinds of recipes without detrimentally affecting your nutritional goals:

AVOCADO The buttery-textured fruit, thinly sliced or cut into dice, adds rich flavor and texture to salads and appetizers. Use no more than ½ to 1 avocado for 4 servings, and make sure it is absolutely ripe for optimum taste and consistency.

BACON A strip or two of crisply cooked bacon drained well on paper towels and then crumbled contributes a smoky flavor and crunchy texture when sprinkled over a dish as a garnish. Consider substituting thinly sliced Canadian bacon, which has less than half the fat of streaky bacon. And rinse bacon well before you cook it, or even parboil it briefly, to reduce its saltiness.

CHEESE Consider using a small amount of cheese as a seasoning rather than as a main ingredient. Most whole-milk cheeses contain less than 10 g of fat per 1 oz; reduced-fat cheeses have far less than that.

CREAM A few tablespoonfuls can add extra richness to a sauce, at the cost of about 5 g of fat per tablespoon of heavy cream.

NUTS Though nuts are high in fat, just a scattering of them—toasted and either left in large pieces or chopped (page 119)—adds crunchy texture and full, rich flavor.

OIL Although 100 percent of any oil's calories derive from fat, the thinnest film of oil in a frying pan will promote browning of foods. In a marinade, sauce or dressing, a little fragrant oil such as olive oil or Asian sesame oil seasons and enriches a dish. Try using a light sprinkling of such oils—just enough to add their unique flavors without too much fat.

Making healthy choices

Eating healthy food begins not in the kitchen or dining room but in the market. Your choice of ingredients is the fundamental step towards a nutritionally balanced diet. Choose fresh seafood, poultry and meat from reputable dealers and use within a few days of purchase. Whenever you can, choose fresh, seasonal, locally grown produce—or better yet, grow as much as possible yourself in a simple kitchen garden.

Choosing Seafood

Seafood offers great variety for eating healthy. Naturally succulent and rich in flavor, it is nevertheless lower in overall fat than meat or poultry, making it an ideal featured ingredient for a first course. What's more, many fish—particularly fattier varieties such as salmon and tuna—contain omega-3 fatty acids, found by some medical studies to play a role in the prevention of heart disease. Even shellfish, which had once been restricted from low-cholesterol diets, have recently been found to contain a type of cholesterol that does not raise blood cholesterol levels.

TYPE OF SEAFOOD

3 oz/90 g Cooked Portion	Calories	Fat (g)	Cholesterol (mg)	Omega-3 (g)	Sodium (mg)
Clams	126	1.7	57	trace	95
Crab (Blue)	87	1.5	85	0.4	237
Halibut	119	2.5	35	0.4	59
Mussels (Blue)	147	3.8	48	2.0	313
Salmon (Coho)	157	6.4	42	2.6	50
Sea Bass	105	2.2	45	0.6	74
Shrimp	84	0.9	166	trace	190
Tuna (white, water-packed)	116	2.1	35	0.6	333

When shopping for any seafood, seek out the most reputable merchant in your area, who has varied selections and a frequent turnover of fresh product. Avoid any seafood that doesn't have a clean, fresh scent of the ocean. Fish should look bright and lustrous, free of discoloration or drying. Shellfish should be either freshly cooked or, in the case of clams and mussels, alive when purchased; avoid or discard any that gape open and do not close tightly when handled. Store fresh seafood securely wrapped in the coldest part of the refrigerator. Aim to cook it within 24 hours of purchase.

CHOOSING BEANS, GRAINS & PASTAS

Grains, pastas and beans seem to have it all for the healthy cook. High in protein and dietary fiber, low in fat and cholesterol free, they satisfy the appetite at a cost significantly lower than the average animal protein. And their wide variety of tastes, textures, colors and shapes lends them to a range of different uses.

Because no single plant source contains all nine of the essential amino acids necessary for good nutrition, grains, pastas and beans should be eaten in complementary combinations—such as the classic pairing of rice and beans—to form complete proteins. Such a need is not so pressing, however, where first courses are concerned; you can use any of these ingredients on its own, just as long as the menu you've planned includes a complementary partner, or some form of animal protein, in another course.

When purchasing beans, look for brightness and uniform size. Different sizes require different cooking times. Store beans in tightly covered glass containers in a cool, dark place and use within a year. The longer a bean is stored, the longer it will take to cook.

When purchasing grains, avoid any with mold. Store whole grains in tightly covered containers in the refrigerator for up to five months or at room temperature for up to one month. To protect grains from insects, add a few bay leaves to the container.

Pasta is available fresh and dried. Store fresh pasta in the refrigerator and cook within a few days. Store dried pasta in tightly covered glass containers in a cool, dark place and use within a year.

TYPE OF GRAIN				
1 CUP (6 OZ/185 G) COOKED	CALORIES	PROTEIN (G)	FAT (G)	CARBOHYDRATE (G)
Barley (Pearl)	193	3.55	0.7	44.0
Bulgur	152	5.60	0.4	34.0
Beans, Black	227	15.20	0.9	40.7
Beans, White	249	17.40	0.6	44.9
Lentils	231	17.90	0.7	39.8
Pasta (Elbow macaroni)	197	6.67	0.9	40.0
Peas, Split	231	16.30	0.8	41.3
RICE				
Long-Grain White	264	5.50	0.6	57.0
Wild	166	6.50	0.6	35.0

CHOOSING FRUITS & VEGETABLES

The classic image of the harvest's horn of plenty sums up the greatest contribution vegetables and fruits make to a healthy diet: abundant variety. With their varied hues, textures and flavors, the produce available to today's shopper provides a wealth of first course possibilities, from dips of roasted vegetables to robust soups to refreshingly crisp and colorful salads.

Although they provide little in the way of protein, vegetables are excellent sources of carbohydrates, water and fiber—as well as generous amounts of vitamins A, B and C and such minerals as calcium, iron and magnesium. Fruits are especially rich in vitamins A and C, complex carbohydrates, natural sugars, fiber and, of course, water.

Buy your fruits and vegetables from the best local source you can find—one that has a wide variety and a frequent turnover of merchandise. Select fruit without mold or bruises, that is neither hard nor soft and mushy. The best indicator of ripe fruit is your nose: smell the fruit, if it smells right, it's probably ready to eat. If you purchase fruit that is not quite ripe, place it in a brown paper bag at room temperature for a few days to ripen without rotting.

Wash fruits and vegetables well and dry them completely before storage. Most fruits and vegetables should be stored in a cool, dark place; others can be refrigerated. In either case, check that the produce remains dry. Even the smallest amount of moisture will quickly turn to mold.

Wash seasonal fruits after purchase and have them on display in the kitchen and dining areas, where their easy access will encourage their use as a healthy snack.

A KITCHEN HERB GARDEN

Fresh herbs add a wonderful lift to the flavor and color of a healthy first course. Whether you live in the city, the suburbs or the country, herbs can be yours for the picking anytime you need them—with a kitchen herb garden.

All you need is a window that gets at least five hours of sunlight daily. Place small pots of herbs on a windowsill or countertop or table, keeping small saucers or a shallow tray under them to catch water. Grow your herbs from seeds or small plants—purchased from the nursery or a garden catalog—in containers of sterile potting soil.

Choose those herbs that you use most often, or try a new one that you've never tasted before.

The most common culinary herbs that grow well indoors are chives, nasturtium, parsley, savory, tarragon and thyme.

Take care not to overwater your herbs; you should keep the soil just moist to the touch. When you need to add one to a recipe, simply pinch off the required amount with your fingertips or snip off a small sprig with kitchen scissors. Use your herbs regularly, and no pruning is necessary!

CHOOSING SALAD GREENS

An ever greater range of salad leaves is becoming available ready to add a wide variety of colors, shapes, tastes and textures to the salad bowl. In addition, leafy vegetables provide good sources of vitamins, including A, C and the B group, as well as various minerals. Purchase crisp greens free of brown spots. Separate the leaves and wash in cold water prior to storage. To remove grit, place in a bowl, add cold water to cover and soak for a few minutes. The leaves will float while the dirt sinks. Drain in a colander and dry with a kitchen towel or use a salad spinner. Store clean, dry greens in the refrigerator.

ARUGULA

Slender, multiple-lobed leaves with a peppery, slightly bitter flavor. Also known as rocket and roquette greens.

BELGIAN ENDIVE

Refreshing, slightly bitter spear-shaped leaves, white to pale yellow green tightly packed in cylindrical heads 4–6 inches (10–15 cm) long. Also known as chicory or witloof.

BUTTER LETTUCE

Relatively small type of round lettuce with soft, loosely packed, tender, mildly flavored leaves. Also known as Boston lettuce. Butter lettuce is a member of the butterhead family, which also includes the Bibb, or limestone, variety.

CHICORY

A relative of Belgian endive, with loosely packed, curly leaves characterized by their bitter flavor. The paler center leaves, or heart, of a head of chicory are milder tasting than the dark-green outer leaves. Also called curly endive.

GREEN-LEAF OR RED-LEAF LETTUCE

Any of a variety of loose-leafed lettuces characterized by their slightly crinkled, medium- to dark-green leaves and by a flavor more pronounced than butter lettuces. Red-leaf lettuces have a dark crimson tone at the tip of each leaf.

RADICCHIO

Leaf vegetable related to Belgian endive. The most common variety has a spherical head, reddish purple leaves with creamy white ribs and a mildly bitter flavor. Other varieties are slightly tapered and vary a bit in color. Also called red chicory.

ROMAINE LETTUCE

Popular variety of lettuce with elongated, pale-green leaves characterized by their crisp texture and slightly pungent flavor. Also called cos lettuce.

SPINACH

Choose smaller, more tender spinach leaves for salads. Be sure to wash thoroughly, in several changes of water, to eliminate all dirt and sand.

WATERCRESS

Refreshing, slightly peppery, dark-green leaf vegetable commercially cultivated and also found wild in freshwater streams.

READING A NUTRITIONAL CHART

Each recipe in this book has been evaluated by a registered dietitian. Beside each recipe, a chart similar to the one below lists the nutrient breakdown per serving. Use these numbers as a tool when putting together meals—and weeks and months of meals—designed for healthy eating.

All ingredients listed within each recipe have been included in the nutritional analysis. Exceptions are items inserted "to taste" and those listed as "optional." When seasoning with salt, bear in mind that you are adding 2,200 mg of sodium for each teaspoon of regular salt and 1,800 mg per teaspoon of coarse kosher or sea salt. The addition of black or white pepper does not alter nutrient values. Substituted ingredients, recipe variations and accompaniments suggested in recipe introductions or shown in photographs have not been included in the analysis.

Quantities are based on a single serving of each recipe.

Protein, one of the basic life-giving nutrients, helps build and repair body tissues and performs other essential functions. One gram of protein contains 4 calories. A healthy diet derives about 15% of daily calories from protein.

Total fat is a measure of the grams of fat present in a serving, with 1 gram of fat equivalent to 9 calories (more than twice the calories in a gram of protein or carbohydrates). Experts recommend that fat intake be limited to a maximum of 30% of total calories.

Cholesterol is present in foods of animal origin. Experts suggest a daily intake of no more than 300 mg. Plant foods contain no cholesterol.

Nutritional Analysis Per Serving:

CALORIES 63
(KILOJOULES 263)
PROTEIN 6 G
CARBOHYDRATES 4 G
TOTAL FAT 2 G
SATURATED FAT 1 G
CHOLESTEROL 16 MG
SODIUM 312 MG
DIETARY FIBER 1 G

Calories (kilojoules) provide a measure of the energy provided by any given food. A calorie equals the heat energy necessary to raise the temperature of 1 kg of water by 1° Celsius. One calorie is equal to 4.2 kilojoules—a term used instead of calories in some countries.

Carbohydrates, classed as either simple (sugars) or complex (starches), are the main source of dietary energy. One gram of carbohydrates contains 4 calories. A healthy diet derives about 55% of calories from carbohydrates, with no more than 10% coming from sugars.

Saturated fat, derived from animal products and some tropical oils, has been found to raise blood cholesterol, and should be limited to no more than one third of total fat calories.

Sodium, derived from salt and naturally present in many foods, helps maintain a proper balance of body fluids. Excess intake can lead to high blood pressure or hypertension in sodium-sensitive people. Those not sensitive should limit intake to about 2,400 mg daily.

Fiber in food aids elimination and helps prevent heart disease, intestinal disease and some forms of cancer. A healthy diet should include 20–35 grams of fiber daily.

A Note on Weights and Measures:
All recipes include customary U.S. and metric measurements. Metric conversions are based on a standard developed for these books and have been rounded off. Actual weights may vary. Unless otherwise stated, the recipes were designed for medium-sized fruits and vegetables.

Appetizers

*P*lump tiger shrimp marinated in a sauce heady with lemon, garlic and mustard; crab cakes topped with a refreshing  grapefruit salsa; a luscious spread of ricotta, tomatoes and fresh basil; skewers of chicken breast grilled with a savory glaze. The recipes in this chapter, although widely varied, share a common goal: to do nothing less than excite the appetite totally while adhering to basic principles of healthy cooking. You'll find no trace of deep-frying or of the ample butter, cream and cheese that were the signatures of so many appetizers of the past. Instead, here, freshness reigns with such quick, lowfat cooking methods as steaming, grilling and broiling and in the use of seasonal produce ranging from bell peppers to Belgian endive, citrus fruits to just-picked herbs. Such variety also bestows great versatility upon these recipes. Use these dishes as they were designed, first courses to a full meal; double or triple them to serve as party hors d'oeuvres or combine several of them to compose an entire healthy, well-balanced meal of many small tastes.

Just a tablespoon of cream enriches the sauce; make it lighter still by substituting 2 tablespoons of Simple Vinaigrette (recipe on page 124). If you pass it at a party, remember a receptacle for the shells. Canned tomato sauce was used in the nutritional analysis.

CHILLED MUSSELS

Serves 6

2 lb (1 kg) mussels
½ cup each (4 fl oz/125 ml) water
  and dry white wine or 1 cup
  (8 fl oz/250 ml) Fish Stock
  (recipe on page 126)
¾ cup (6 fl oz/180 ml) tomato sauce
⅛ teaspoon saffron threads
1 tablespoon heavy (double) cream
2 tablespoons chopped fresh parsley

*Nutritional Analysis
Per Serving:*

CALORIES 63
(KILOJOULES 263)
PROTEIN 6 G
CARBOHYDRATES 4 G
TOTAL FAT 2 G
SATURATED FAT 1 G
CHOLESTEROL 16 MG
SODIUM 312 MG
DIETARY FIBER 1 G

1. To determine the freshness of mussels, press the shell of each one between your thumb and forefinger. If it does not close tightly to the touch, discard it. Soak the mussels in cold water to cover for 15 minutes. Pull the beard away from each shell and brush the mussels vigorously under cold running water to remove excess sand. Again, soak the mussels in cold water to cover for 15 minutes. Drain and scrub under cold running water to remove sand.

2. In a stockpot, bring the water and wine or Fish Stock to a boil over high heat. Add the mussels, cover tightly and cook over high heat, occasionally shaking the pot vigorously by its handles so the mussels cook evenly. When the mussels have opened, in about 5 minutes, remove from the heat immediately and let cool. Discard any unopened mussels.

3. Line a sieve with cheesecloth (muslin) and strain ¼ cup (2 fl oz/60 ml) of the cooking liquid to remove any sand.

4. Remove the top shell from each mussel and discard. Place the mussels in their bottom shells on a large platter, arranging them in concentric circles.

5. In a frying pan over medium heat, combine the strained cooking liquid, the tomato sauce, saffron and cream. Bring to a boil and boil until reduced to ¾ cup (6 fl oz/180 ml), about 5 minutes. Pour over the mussels, cover and refrigerate for at least 2 hours and up to 8 hours.

6. To serve, garnish with the parsley and serve chilled.

Let guests help themselves from this attractive buffet table or picnic dish, mounding the spread onto crackers and topping it with sun-dried tomato salsa. To keep fat at a minimum, choose lowfat crackers.

Ricotta & Goat Cheese Spread

Serves 6

1 cup (8 oz/250 g) lowfat ricotta cheese

3 oz (90 g) fresh goat cheese

⅓ cup (3 oz/85 g) sun-dried tomatoes, dry-packed

2 garlic cloves, peeled and minced

1 shallot, finely chopped

½ lb (250 g) plum (Roma) tomatoes (about 2), peeled, seeded and diced

¼ cup (¼ oz/7 g) chopped fresh basil leaves

½ teaspoon fresh thyme leaves

2 tablespoons olive oil

¼ teaspoon salt

⅛ teaspoon freshly ground pepper

small fresh basil leaves

18 lowfat whole-wheat (wholemeal) crackers

1. In a food processor fitted with the metal blade, combine the ricotta and goat cheeses. Process until softened and completely blended. Transfer to a serving bowl, cover and refrigerate.

2. To make the salsa, place the sun-dried tomatoes in a heatproof bowl and add boiling water to cover. Let stand until softened and very pliable, 25–30 minutes. Drain, squeeze dry and chop coarsely.

3. In a bowl, combine the sun-dried tomatoes, garlic, shallot, plum tomatoes, basil and thyme. Add the olive oil, salt and pepper and toss until well blended. Cover and refrigerate until serving, up to 8 hours.

4. To serve, mound the cheese on a serving platter. Spoon the salsa around the edge of the cheese mound. Garnish with basil leaves. Serve with the crackers.

Nutritional Analysis Per Serving:

CALORIES 194
(KILOJOULES 813)
PROTEIN 10 G
CARBOHYDRATES 15 G
TOTAL FAT 12 G
SATURATED FAT 5 G
CHOLESTEROL 18 MG
SODIUM 316 MG
DIETARY FIBER 2 G

Triangles of warm quesadilla have a place on the healthy table when made with lowfat cheese and heated in a nonstick pan. Corn tortillas contain less fat than the flour ones. Each serving consists of 2 quesadilla halves, a teaspoon of sour cream and a cilantro sprig.

Quesadillas

Serves 4

8 large sun-dried tomatoes, dry-packed
4 lowfat corn or flour tortillas
1 cup (4 oz/125 g) shredded lowfat mozzarella cheese
8 teaspoons minced red (Spanish) onion
4 teaspoons lowfat sour cream
8 fresh cilantro (fresh coriander) sprigs

Nutritional Analysis Per Serving:

Calories 176
(Kilojoules 737)
Protein 10 g
Carbohydrates 21 g
Total Fat 7 g
Saturated Fat 3 g
Cholesterol 18 mg
Sodium 191 mg
Dietary Fiber 4 g

1. Place the sun-dried tomatoes in a heatproof bowl and add boiling water to cover. Let stand until softened and very pliable, 25–30 minutes. Drain, squeeze dry and slice into long, thin strips. Set aside.
2. On a flat surface, lay out the 4 tortillas. Spoon one-fourth of the shredded cheese over the lower half of 1 tortilla, leaving a 1-inch (2.5-cm) border around the edge. Spoon 2 teaspoons of the minced onion over the cheese and then top with one fourth of the sun-dried tomato strips. Repeat with the remaining tortillas, cheese and onion.
3. Heat a nonstick frying pan or griddle over medium-high heat. When it is hot, away from the fire, lightly coat with nonstick cooking spray. Slip the first tortilla into the pan. Fold the un-covered half over to cover the cheese mixture, pressing down with a spatula.
4. Cook the quesadilla until lightly browned on the first side, about 2 minutes. Turn the quesadilla over and cook the other side, pressing down occasionally with the spatula, until lightly browned as well, another 2 minutes. Using the spatula, transfer to a cutting board and cut in half to make 2 triangles. Cover with aluminum foil to keep warm and cook the remaining 3 quesadillas in the same manner.
5. To serve, arrange the quesadilla halves, sour cream and cilantro on a serving platter.

A specialty throughout Latin America, ceviche calls for fish or shellfish to be marinated in citrus juice. The citrus acid firms up the seafood and turns it opaque much as cooking would. The result is a fresh-tasting warm-weather appetizer.

SCALLOP CEVICHE & SALSA

Serves 4

4 limes
½ lb (250 g) bay scallops or sea scallops cut into ½-inch (12-mm) pieces
½ cup (4 fl oz/125 ml) fresh lemon juice
½ teaspoon salt
¼ teaspoon red pepper flakes
2 tablespoons minced red (Spanish) onion

3 plum (Roma) tomatoes, peeled, seeded and cut into ¼-inch (6-mm) dice
2 green (spring) onions, green and white parts, finely chopped
1 tablespoon finely chopped fresh cilantro (fresh coriander)
1 tablespoon olive oil
¼ teaspoon salt
⅛ teaspoon freshly ground pepper
1 head butter lettuce, separated into leaves

1. Remove the zest in long, fine strips from 1 lime and set the zest aside to use in the salsa. Halve the limes and squeeze as needed to measure ½ cup (4 fl oz/125 ml) juice.
2. In a shallow, nonreactive dish, combine the scallops, lime juice, lemon juice, salt, red pepper flakes and red onion. Toss well. If the liquid does not completely cover the scallops, add more as necessary to cover. Cover the dish with plastic wrap and refrigerate for at least 4 hours or for up to 6 hours. The scallops should become opaque.
3. To make the salsa, in a medium bowl, combine the tomatoes, green onions, cilantro, the reserved lime zest, olive oil, salt and pepper. Stir to mix well, cover and refrigerate for up to 1 hour.
4. Drain the scallops, discarding the marinade. Add the scallops to the bowl with the salsa and toss to mix well.
5. To serve, place a few lettuce leaves on individual plates. Mound one fourth of the scallop-salsa mixture onto each portion.

Nutritional Analysis Per Serving:

**CALORIES 99
(KILOJOULES 417)
PROTEIN 11 G
CARBOHYDRATES 6 G
TOTAL FAT 4 G
SATURATED FAT 1 G
CHOLESTEROL 19 MG
SODIUM 302 MG
DIETARY FIBER 1 G**

In this easy but impressive dish, spear-shaped leaves of Belgian endive become edible containers for a light, fresh-tasting salad of sweet, tender bay shrimp. Tightly closed, pale yellow-green spears of endive will have the best flavor.

Dilled Shrimp on Belgian Endive

Serves 6

2 heads Belgian endive
  (chicory/witloof)
½ cup (4 fl oz/125 ml) Simple
  Vinaigrette *(recipe on page 124)*
½ English (hothouse) cucumber,
  unpeeled, halved lengthwise and
  cut into ⅛-inch (3-mm) dice
¼ lb (125 g) cooked bay shrimp
  (about ½ cup), coarsely chopped

2 tablespoons finely chopped
  fresh dill
1 tablespoon finely chopped red
  (Spanish) onion
⅛ teaspoon salt
⅛ teaspoon coarsely ground pepper
English (hothouse) cucumber slices,
  optional
dill sprigs, optional

1. Separate the endive spears. As you get closer to the center, you may have to trim more from the bottom in order to free the spears.

2. In a nonreactive bowl, combine the Simple Vinaigrette, diced cucumber, shrimp, chopped dill, red onion, salt and pepper and stir to mix well.

3. To serve, scoop about 2 teaspoons of the dill-shrimp relish onto the end of each spear. Arrange the spears on individual plates and garnish with the cucumber slices and dill sprigs, if used.

Nutritional Analysis Per Serving:

**Calories 100
(Kilojoules 420)
Protein 4 g
Carbohydrates 2 g
Total Fat 8 g
Saturated Fat 1 g
Cholesterol 37 mg
Sodium 168 mg
Dietary Fiber 1 g**

Tart, zesty grapefruit provides an excellent counterpoint to the natural sweetness of crab meat. This recipe was designed, and the nutritional analysis performed, with fresh Dungeness crab, however, cooked and frozen or other types of crab can be substituted.

OVEN-BAKED CRAB CAKES

Serves 4

1 egg
½ teaspoon Dijon-style mustard
⅛ teaspoon salt
⅛ teaspoon cayenne pepper
1½ teaspoons finely chopped
  fresh chives

½ lb (250 g) Dungeness crab meat, pulled
  apart into ½-inch (12-mm) chunks
¼ cup (1 oz/30 g) fresh bread crumbs
¼ cup (1 oz/30 g) fine dried bread crumbs
½ pink grapefruit
4 red-leaf lettuce leaves
¼ cup (2 fl oz/60 ml) Simple Vinaigrette
  (recipe on page 124)

1. In a mixing bowl, whisk the egg until blended. Add the mustard, salt, cayenne pepper and chives and mix to incorporate. Add the crab meat and the fresh bread crumbs and whisk to mix well.
2. Preheat an oven to 425°F (220°C).
3. Spread the dried bread crumbs on a baking sheet. Divide the crab mixture into 4 equal portions. Shape each portion into a cake about 3 inches (7.5 cm) in diameter and ¾ inch (2 cm) thick, pressing out as much liquid as possible to form compact cakes. Coat the crab cakes completely with the dried bread crumbs, using a spatula, turn and then transfer them to a large plate. Cover with plastic wrap and refrigerate for at least 1 hour or for up to 6 hours. (The chilling helps to keep the cakes together when they are cooking.)
4. Lightly coat a nonstick frying pan with nonstick cooking spray and place over medium-high heat. When the pan is hot, add the crab cakes and sauté, turning once, until golden brown on both sides, 1–2 minutes on each side. Use a flat-bottomed spatula for easy turning. Transfer the crab cakes to a baking sheet and bake in the oven until puffed and brown, 7–8 minutes.

Nutritional Analysis Per Serving:

CALORIES 170
(KILOJOULES 716)
PROTEIN 13 G
CARBOHYDRATES 10 G
TOTAL FAT 9 G
SATURATED FAT 1 G
CHOLESTEROL 87 MG
SODIUM 402 MG
DIETARY FIBER 0 G

5. Meanwhile, peel the grapefruit half, removing all the white pith. Using a sharp knife, cut alongside the segments to release them from the membrane. Remove any seeds, then chop the segments.

6. To serve, place 1 lettuce leaf in the center of individual plates. Spoon an equal quantity of the chopped grapefruit onto each leaf. Place 1 crab cake on top of each portion of grapefruit. Spoon an equal portion of the Simple Vinaigrette over the top of and around the cakes.

A light, lemony marinade seasoned with garlic, mustard and red pepper flakes makes this lively dish a refreshing alternative to the traditional shrimp cocktail. Pass it at a party, remembering a receptacle for the tails, or plate it as a first course.

CITRUS-MARINATED SHRIMP

Serves 6

1 cup (8 fl oz/250 ml) each water and dry white wine or 2 cups (16 fl oz/500 ml) Fish Stock *(recipe on page 126)*

1 bay leaf, if using water-wine mixture

1 lb (500 g) large or medium shrimp (prawns) (14–16 large or about 30 medium), peeled, with tail fin segment intact, and deveined

1 small red bell pepper (capsicum), seeded, deribbed, thinly sliced and cut into ¼-inch (6-mm) widths by 2-inch (5-cm) lengths

1 small red (Spanish) onion, thinly sliced (about ¾ cup/3 oz/90g)

½ cup (2½ oz/75 g) Kalamata olives, pitted and halved

1 lemon, peeled and thinly sliced

½ cup (4 fl oz/125 ml) fresh lemon juice

¼ cup (2 fl oz/60 ml) olive oil

1 tablespoon red wine vinegar

1 garlic clove, peeled and minced

1 tablespoon mustard powder

red pepper flakes

½ teaspoon salt

⅛ teaspoon coarsely cracked pepper

1 tablespoon finely chopped fresh parsley

red-leaf lettuce leaves

Nutritional Analysis Per Serving:

CALORIES 166
(KILOJOULES 698)
PROTEIN 13 G
CARBOHYDRATES 7 G
TOTAL FAT 9 G
SATURATED FAT 1 G
CHOLESTEROL 93 MG
SODIUM 335 MG
DIETARY FIBER 1 G

1. In a 2-qt (2-l) saucepan, place the water and wine or Fish Stock. Add the bay leaf, if using, and bring to a boil. Add the shrimp. Cover, reduce the heat to low and cook, stirring occasionally, until the shrimp are pink and cooked in the center, 3–5 minutes. Using a slotted spoon, transfer the shrimp to a bowl.

2. Add the bell pepper to the shrimp cooking liquid and simmer over medium heat for 1 minute. Using a slotted spoon, transfer to the bowl holding the shrimp. Discard the cooking liquid. Add the onion, olives and lemon slices to the shrimp and toss gently to mix.

3. To make the marinade, in a bowl, whisk to combine the lemon juice, olive oil, red wine vinegar, garlic, mustard powder, pepper flakes, salt, pepper and parsley. Pour over the shrimp mixture. Refrigerate for 4–8 hours.

4. To serve, line a plate with lettuce leaves and, using a slotted spoon, place the shrimp on top. Drizzle with ½ cup (4 fl oz/125 ml) of the marinade.

Black beans have a naturally earthy flavor and rich texture that make them an ideal candidate for transforming into a healthy, satisfying dip. The accompanying oven-baked chips are considerably lower in fat than deep-fried commercial brands.

Spicy Black Bean Dip & Tortilla Chips

Serves 6

2 cups (14 oz/440 g) well-drained home-cooked or canned black beans, rinsed

¼ cup (2 fl oz/60 ml) Poultry Stock *(recipe on page 127)*

½ red bell pepper (capsicum), seeded, deribbed and very finely diced

1 small fresh jalapeño chili pepper, minced

2 teaspoons tequila

1 teaspoon fresh lime juice

½ teaspoon dried oregano

¼ teaspoon salt

⅛ teaspoon coarsely cracked black pepper

2 tablespoons olive oil

6 corn tortillas, each cut into 6 triangles

salt and freshly ground pepper

¼ cup (2 fl oz/60 ml) lowfat sour cream

fresh cilantro (fresh coriander) sprigs

1. Preheat an oven to 400°F (200°C).

2. To make the dip, in a food processor fitted with the metal blade, place 1½ cups (10½ oz/330 g) of the beans. Process to a paste, adding the Poultry Stock to keep the mixture moving in the processor. Do not thin too much; it should be a thick paste.

3. In a mixing bowl, combine the black bean paste with the remaining ½ cup (3½ oz/110 g) of whole beans, the bell pepper, jalapeño pepper, tequila, lime juice, oregano, salt, black pepper and olive oil. Stir to mix well. You should have about 2¼ cups (18 fl oz/560 ml). Cover and refrigerate until needed.

4. To make the tortilla chips, place the tortilla triangles on a baking sheet. Place in the oven and bake until crisp, about 10 minutes. Remove from the oven. Sprinkle with the salt and pepper to taste.

5. To serve, mound the bean dip in a medium-sized serving bowl and garnish with the sour cream and cilantro sprigs. Place the bowl in the center of a large platter and arrange the warm tortilla chips around the edge.

Nutritional Analysis Per Serving:

Calories 190
(Kilojoules 799)
Protein 7 g
Carbohydrates 27 g
Total Fat 6 g
Saturated Fat 1 g
Cholesterol 3 mg
Sodium 141 mg
Dietary Fiber 3 g

Baking in the oven develops a creamy texture in eggplant, featured here in a variation on a favorite Middle Eastern appetizer. Serve the dip with the crackers, lightly toasted slices of French bread, hot wedges of pita bread or crisp raw vegetables.

Roasted Eggplant Dip

Serves 6

2 plum (Roma) tomatoes, peeled, seeded and cut into ½-inch (12-mm) dice
3 tablespoons balsamic vinegar
3 tablespoons olive oil
3 shallots, finely chopped
1 garlic clove, peeled and minced
¼ teaspoon salt
¼ teaspoon pepper

3 eggplants (aubergines), 3 lb (1.5 kg) total weight, peeled and cut into 1½-inch (4-cm) pieces
⅓ cup (⅓ oz/10 g) finely chopped fresh basil leaves
12 Kalamata olives
fresh basil leaves
24 lowfat whole-wheat (wholemeal) crackers

Nutritional Analysis Per Serving:

1. Preheat an oven to 400°F (200°C).
2. In a bowl, combine the tomatoes, 1 tablespoon of the balsamic vinegar and 1 tablespoon of the olive oil. Stir to mix well; set aside.
3. Lightly coat a large roasting pan with nonstick cooking spray. In the prepared pan, combine the shallots, garlic, 1 more tablespoon of the balsamic vinegar, the remaining 2 tablespoons olive oil and the salt and pepper. Add the eggplant and toss to coat evenly. Roast, stirring every 15 minutes so it will cook evenly, until the eggplant is very soft, 1–1¼ hours.
4. Remove from the oven and let cool. Add the remaining 1 tablespoon balsamic vinegar and the chopped basil and stir to mix well.
5. To serve, mound on a serving dish and garnish with the tomato mixture, olives and basil leaves. Serve with the crackers.

Calories 168
(Kilojoules 705)
Protein 3 g
Carbohydrates 24 g
Total Fat 8 g
Saturated Fat 1 g
Cholesterol 0 mg
Sodium 294 mg
Dietary Fiber 4 g

Though high-fat ingredients have been kept to a minimum here, the combination of intensely flavored sun-dried tomatoes and freshly grated Parmesan cheese in these classic Italian toasts nonetheless brings to mind a pizza.

Sun-Dried Tomato Parmesan Chips

Serves 6

⅓ cup (2 oz/57 g) sun-dried
   tomatoes, dry-packed
20 slices French or sourdough bread,
   each about 2½ inches (6 cm) in
   diameter and ¼ inch (6 mm) thick

3 tablespoons olive oil
¼ cup (1 oz/30 g) freshly grated
   Parmesan cheese

1. Place the sun-dried tomatoes in a heatproof bowl and add boiling water to cover. Let stand until softened and very pliable, 30 minutes. Drain and place in a food processor fitted with the metal blade. Process, scraping down the bowl as necessary and adding a little hot water, 1 teaspoon at a time, as needed to form a paste.

2. Preheat an oven to 375°F (190°C). Place the bread slices on a baking sheet and bake until dry and firm but not golden, about 5 minutes. Remove and let cool. Leave the oven set at 375°F (190°C).

3. In a small bowl, combine the olive oil and the sun-dried tomato paste and stir to mix well. Spread each piece of toast with an equal amount of the tomato mixture. Sprinkle with the Parmesan cheese.

4. Bake until the cheese melts but is not browned, about 5 minutes. Watch carefully so they do not burn. Remove from the oven, let cool and serve. If not using immediately, store the chips in a tightly covered container at room temperature for up to 3 days.

*Nutritional Analysis
Per Serving:*

**Calories 150
(Kilojoules 628)
Protein 4 g
Carbohydrates 14 g
Total Fat 9 g
Saturated Fat 2 g
Cholesterol 3 mg
Sodium 209 mg
Dietary Fiber 2 g**

A marinade of orange juice, honey, mustard and low sodium soy sauce adds beguiling flavor to chunks of skinless chicken breast in these little broiled or grilled kabobs. If using wooden skewers, presoak them in water for 30 minutes to prevent burning.

ORANGE-MUSTARD GLAZED CHICKEN

Serves 6

3 chicken breast halves, skinned, boned and cut into ¾-inch (2-cm) cubes (12 oz/375 g total weight when boned)
½ cup (4 fl oz/125 ml) fresh orange juice
1 shallot, finely chopped
2 tablespoons honey
1 tablespoon Dijon-style mustard
1 teaspoon low sodium soy sauce
2 teaspoons olive oil
¼ teaspoon salt
⅛ teaspoon freshly ground pepper
finely shredded zest of 1 orange

1. In a nonreactive bowl, combine the chicken, orange juice, shallot, honey, mustard, soy sauce, olive oil, salt and pepper. Toss to coat the chicken well. Cover and refrigerate for at least 2 hours but for no longer than 5 hours.
2. Preheat a broiler (griller) or a gas or electric grill.
3. Using a slotted spoon, remove the chicken from the bowl, reserving the marinade. Thread an equal amount of chicken onto each of 6 skewers. Lay each filled skewer on a platter lined with paper towels and turn gently to remove the excess marinade. Place the reserved marinade in a small saucepan and boil over medium-high heat until reduced by half and thickened to a glaze, about 5 minutes.
4. Place the skewers on a broiling pan or on a grill rack and broil or grill about 1½ minutes on each of all 4 sides, for a total of 6 minutes, or until the chicken is cooked through with no trace of pink remaining.
5. To serve, place the skewers on a serving platter. Drizzle with the glaze and sprinkle with the orange zest.

Nutritional Analysis Per Serving:

CALORIES 111
(KILOJOULES 465)
PROTEIN 13 G
CARBOHYDRATES 9 G
TOTAL FAT 2 G
SATURATED FAT 0 G
CHOLESTEROL 32 MG
SODIUM 236 MG
DIETARY FIBER 0 G

Soups

Scientific studies recently found that people who start a meal with soup find it easier to control their weight. Such findings come as no surprise to those who love soup. Savored spoonful  by spoonful, soup prolongs a meal. Eating slowly, we tend to eat less. In short, soup satisfies. The recipes that follow offer satisfaction and good nutrition in abundance. They range from cool concoctions ideal for a summer's day to heart-warming chowders ready to chase away winter's chill. Many are ready to move from the introductory spot on the menu to main dish status, needing only a simple salad and bread to become a light yet filling lunch. Whether cold or hot, briefly boiled or slowly simmered, all these soups are easy to assemble, their ingredients requiring for the most part just some simple cutting, slicing or chopping before they are thrown together in the stockpot or food processor. Many can be made ahead, refrigerated or frozen and then heated when needed. For the health-conscious but busy cook, what could possibly be more satisfying?

San Francisco's signature soup is ideal as a first course or casual main dish, accompanied by Garlic Toasts and salad. To make a bouquet garni, place the parsley stem, bay leaf and thyme sprig on a small square of cheesecloth (muslin), bring the corners together and tie securely.

CIOPPINO WITH GARLIC TOASTS

Serves 8

1 fresh parsley stem
1 bay leaf
1 fresh thyme sprig
3 tablespoons olive oil
2 celery stalks, finely chopped
1 yellow onion, finely chopped
1 carrot, peeled and finely chopped
1½ lb (750 g) fresh tomatoes, peeled and coarsely chopped
¼ cup (2 fl oz/60 ml) tomato paste
3 tablespoons fresh lemon juice
3 garlic cloves, peeled and minced
3½ cups (28 fl oz/875 ml) Fish Stock *(recipe on page 126)*

2 cups (16 fl oz/500 ml) fruity red wine, such as Zinfandel
¼ teaspoon sugar
1 teaspoon fennel seeds
2 lb (1 kg) white fish, such as sea bass or halibut, cut into ¾-inch (2-cm) pieces
16 clams in the shell, well scrubbed
16 mussels in the shell, well scrubbed

GARLIC TOASTS
16 French or Italian bread slices, each 3 inches (7.5 cm) in diameter and ½ inch (12 mm) thick
1 garlic clove, peeled and halved
3 tablespoons finely chopped fresh parsley

Nutritional Analysis Per Serving:

CALORIES 362
(KILOJOULES 1,522)
PROTEIN 32 G
CARBOHYDRATES 33 G
TOTAL FAT 11 G
SATURATED FAT 2 G
CHOLESTEROL 61 MG
SODIUM 582 MG
DIETARY FIBER 3 G

1. In a large, nonreactive stockpot over medium heat, warm the olive oil. Add the celery, onion and carrot and sauté, stirring occasionally, until softened, about 5 minutes. Add the tomatoes, tomato paste, lemon juice, garlic, Fish Stock, wine, sugar, fennel seeds and bouquet garni (see introductory text). Cover partially and simmer over medium-low heat until slightly reduced, about 40 minutes.

2. Prepare the Garlic Toasts (see opposite page).

3. Add the fish to the stockpot, cover and simmer over medium heat for 3 minutes. Discard all open, uncooked clams and mussels. Add the closed clams and mussels, cover and simmer until the shellfish open and the fish is just cooked through, 5 minutes longer.

4. Remove and discard the bouquet garni and any unopened shellfish.

5. To serve, ladle into individual bowls, being sure to divide the seafood evenly. Serve 2 Garlic Toasts alongside each bowl.

GARLIC TOASTS

1. Preheat an oven to 375°F (190°C).

2. Place the bread slices on a baking sheet and bake until just golden, 5–7 minutes; watch carefully that they do not burn.

3. Rub each slice with the cut side of a garlic clove, and then sprinkle each with an equal amount of the parsley.

The flavors of lentils and meat go nicely together. But, if you'd prefer a vegetarian version, simply replace the beef stock with vegetable stock. For a smoother soup, purée half of it in a food processor or blender and stir back into the pan.

CURRIED LENTIL SOUP

Serves 6

1½ tablespoons olive oil
1 yellow onion, finely chopped
1 celery stalk, thinly sliced
1 carrot, peeled, halved lengthwise
  and thinly sliced
1 garlic clove, peeled and minced
1 bay leaf
1 cup (6 oz/185 g) canned plum
  (Roma) tomatoes, with their juice

2 teaspoons curry powder
1½ cups (10½ oz/330 g) brown
  lentils, picked over and rinsed
6 cups (48 fl oz/1.5 l) Beef Stock
  (recipe on page 126)
1 cup (1 oz/30 g) fresh spinach
  leaves, coarsely chopped
salt and freshly ground pepper

1. In a saucepan over medium heat, warm the olive oil. Add the onion, celery, carrot, garlic and bay leaf and sauté until softened, about 5 minutes.
2. Add the tomatoes and their juice, the curry powder, lentils and Beef Stock to the pan. Bring to a simmer, cover partially and cook over medium-low heat, stirring occasionally, until the lentils are tender, about 30 minutes.
3. Five minutes before serving, stir in the spinach and simmer over low heat. Remove and discard the bay leaf. Add the salt and pepper to taste. Stir to mix well.
4. To serve, ladle into individual bowls.

Nutritional Analysis Per Serving:

CALORIES 242
(KILOJOULES 1,017)
PROTEIN 16 G
CARBOHYDRATES 37 G
TOTAL FAT 4 G
SATURATED FAT 1 G
CHOLESTEROL 0 MG
SODIUM 92 MG
DIETARY FIBER 7 G

Carrot, celery and onion, briefly simmered in the stock, impart fresh flavor to a quick Italian standby—a good opener to almost any Italian menu. Though only 1 egg is used for 4 portions, you can reduce the fat further by substituting 2 egg whites.

Quick Spinach Stracciatella

Serves 4

4 cups (32 fl oz/1 l) Poultry Stock *(recipe on page 127)*

1 carrot, peeled and cut into 2-inch (5-cm) lengths

1 celery stalk, cut into 2-inch (5-cm) lengths

½ small yellow onion, cut into slices ¼ inch (6 mm) thick

4 cups (8 oz/250 g) spinach leaves, stems removed and coarsely chopped

⅛ teaspoon salt

⅛ teaspoon freshly ground pepper

1 egg, beaten

4 teaspoons freshly grated Parmesan cheese, optional

1. In a saucepan over medium-high heat, bring the Poultry Stock to a simmer. Add the carrot, celery and onion and simmer for 10 minutes, to flavor the stock. Using a slotted spoon, lift out the vegetables and reserve them for another use.

2. Fill a small saucepan three-fourths full of water and bring to a boil. Add the spinach and cook until wilted, about 1 minute. Drain and set aside.

3. Raise the heat under the soup to high and bring the soup to a boil. Immediately add the salt, pepper and egg and stir until well distributed in the soup and cooked, about 30 seconds. Remove from the heat.

4. To serve, place an equal amount of the cooked spinach in individual deep soup bowls. Ladle the hot soup over the top. Garnish each serving with 1 teaspoon Parmesan cheese, if using.

Nutritional Analysis Per Serving:

Calories 65
(Kilojoules 274)
Protein 5 g
Carbohydrates 6 g
Total Fat 3 g
Saturated Fat 1 g
Cholesterol 53 mg
Sodium 172 mg
Dietary Fiber 2 g

A refreshing first course for a warm afternoon, this uncooked soup gets its inspiration from the Indian dish known as *raita*. Try adding chopped red onion, diced seeded tomato or shredded carrot. Almonds, pecans or hazelnuts can replace the walnuts.

CHILLED CUCUMBER & YOGURT SOUP

Serves 4

3 cucumbers, peeled, halved lengthwise, seeded and cut into 2-inch (5-cm) lengths

1½ cups (12 oz/375 g) lowfat plain yogurt

1 cup (8 fl oz/250 ml) lowfat buttermilk

1 tablespoon olive oil

1 garlic clove, peeled and minced

3 tablespoons finely chopped fresh chives

2 tablespoons finely chopped fresh dill

⅛ teaspoon red pepper flakes

½ cup (4 fl oz/125 ml) water

½ teaspoon salt

⅛ teaspoon white pepper

2 walnuts, shelled, toasted and chopped coarsely

1. In a food processor fitted with the metal blade, purée half of the cucumber, scraping down the sides of the bowl as necessary, until smooth but not watery, about 20 seconds.

2. In a bowl, combine the puréed cucumber, yogurt, buttermilk, olive oil, garlic, chives, dill and pepper flakes. Stir to mix well.

3. Cut the remaining cucumber into ⅛-inch (3-mm) dice. Stir into the purée mixture. Stir in just enough of the water to give the soup a thin but not watery consistency. Add the salt and pepper and stir to mix well. Refrigerate until well chilled.

4. To serve, ladle into individual bowls. Garnish with the walnuts.

Nutritional Analysis Per Serving:

CALORIES 158
(KILOJOULES 663)
PROTEIN 8 G
CARBOHYDRATES 15 G
TOTAL FAT 8 G
SATURATED FAT 2 G
CHOLESTEROL 8 MG
SODIUM 409 MG
DIETARY FIBER 1 G

The beans and pasta together provide a complete source of protein as well as generous carbohydrates, making this lowfat but hearty soup an excellent alternative main dish for a light lunch when served with toasted French bread slices.

Bean, Pasta & Zucchini Soup

Serves 4

¾ cup (5 oz/155 g) dried Great Northern or cannellini beans, picked over and rinsed

1½ tablespoons olive oil

2 small or 1 medium yellow onion, coarsely chopped

1 carrot, peeled and chopped

5 cups (40 fl oz/1.25 l) Poultry Stock *(recipe on page 127)*

1 garlic clove, peeled and minced

¾ cup (4½ oz/140 g) coarsely chopped, peeled tomatoes (fresh or canned, with their juices)

2 tablespoons finely chopped fresh basil or 2 teaspoons dried basil

1 cup (2 oz/57 g) dried egg noodles, cut into 3-inch (7.5-cm) long pieces

1 cup (5 oz/155 g) shredded zucchini (courgette)

½ teaspoon salt

¼ teaspoon white pepper

2 tablespoons finely chopped fresh parsley

3 tablespoons freshly grated Parmesan cheese, optional

Nutritional Analysis Per Serving:

Calories 308
(Kilojoules 1,293)
Protein 15 g
Carbohydrates 47 g
Total Fat 8 g
Saturated Fat 1 g
Cholesterol 9 mg
Sodium 353 mg
Dietary Fiber 20 g

1. Place the beans in a large bowl with cold water to cover generously and let stand for at least 4 hours. Alternatively, in a saucepan, combine the beans with water to cover, bring to a boil and boil for 2 minutes; remove from the heat, cover and let stand for 1 hour. Drain the beans.

2. In a nonreactive saucepan over medium heat, warm the olive oil. Add the onions and sauté, stirring occasionally, until just wilted, about 5 minutes. Add the carrot and sauté, stirring, for 3 minutes longer. Add the Poultry Stock, the drained beans, garlic, tomatoes and basil and stir to mix well. Cover partially and simmer until the beans are tender, about 1 hour.

3. Fill a saucepan three-fourths full of water and bring to a boil. Add the noodles and cook until tender, 3–5 minutes, or according to package directions. Drain well.

4. In a food processor fitted with the metal blade, purée the soup, leaving the vegetables with some of their texture.

5. Return the soup to the pot and place over medium-high heat. Add the noodles and zucchini and cook for 5 minutes longer. Stir in the salt, pepper and half of the parsley.

6. To serve, ladle into individual bowls. Garnish with an equal amount of the remaining parsley and Parmesan cheese, if using.

Robust as this delicatessen-style soup may taste, it is very low in fat. The barley provides a good source of both complex carbohydrates and iron. If you can't find dried porcini mushrooms, substitute any dried variety.

Mushroom & Barley Soup

Serves 8

2 large garlic cloves, peeled and minced

2 yellow onions, finely chopped

1 leek, green and white parts, coarsely chopped

½ cup (3 oz/90 g) barley

8 cups (64 fl oz/2 l) Beef Stock *(recipe on page 126)*

2 celery stalks, coarsely chopped

2 carrots, peeled and coarsely chopped

1½ cups (4½ oz/140 g) coarsely chopped fresh button mushrooms

¼ cup (½ oz/15 g) dried porcini mushrooms, soaked in ½ cup (4 fl oz/125 ml) hot water for 30 minutes

3 tablespoons finely chopped parsley

salt and freshly ground pepper

1. In a large saucepan over medium-high heat, combine the garlic, onions, leek, barley and Beef Stock. Bring to a simmer and cook for 5 minutes. Add the celery, carrots and button mushrooms, cover and simmer over medium heat until the barley is tender but not mushy, about 1½–2 hours.

2. Drain the porcini mushrooms, reserving the soaking liquid and squeezing the mushrooms well. Cut the porcini into ¼-inch (6-mm) cubes and set aside.

3. Line a sieve with cheesecloth (muslin) and pour the reserved soaking liquid through it to remove any grit. Add it with the porcini mushrooms and parsley to the saucepan. Simmer for 5 minutes longer. Add the salt and pepper to taste.

4. To serve, ladle into individual bowls.

Nutritional Analysis Per Serving:

Calories 102 (Kilojoules 426)
Protein 4 g
Carbohydrates 21 g
Total Fat 1 g
Saturated Fat 0 g
Cholesterol 0 mg
Sodium 29 mg
Dietary Fiber 4 g

French bistros top their onion soup with a thick layer of melted cheese. In this version, a lighter, cheese-topped crouton captures the traditional flavors. Take care to caramelize the onions and leeks slowly to achieve the richest results.

Onion Soup & Gruyère Croutons

Serves 4

2 tablespoons canola oil or olive oil

3 medium or 2 large red (Spanish) onions, thinly sliced

¼ teaspoon sugar

4 leeks, white part only, carefully washed and thinly sliced

6 cups (48 fl oz/1.5 l) Poultry Stock or Beef Stock *(recipes on pages 126–127)*

2 garlic cloves, peeled and minced

1 bay leaf

½ cup (4 fl oz/125 ml) dry white wine

½ teaspoon salt

⅛ teaspoon freshly ground pepper

½ teaspoon minced fresh thyme or ¼ teaspoon dried thyme

12 French or sourdough bread slices, each 3 inches (7.5 cm) in diameter and ¼ inch (6 mm) thick

½ cup (2 oz/60 g) shredded Gruyère cheese

2 tablespoons finely chopped fresh parsley

1. In a large, nonreactive saucepan over medium heat, warm the oil. Add the red onions and sauté, stirring, until wilted, about 15 minutes. Add the sugar and leeks and continue to sauté, stirring frequently, until caramelized, 30–45 minutes.

2. Add the Poultry or Beef Stock, garlic, bay leaf and white wine and stir to mix well. Cover partially and simmer over medium-low heat for an additional 30 minutes. Add the salt, pepper and thyme and stir to mix well. Remove and discard the bay leaf.

3. Just before the soup is ready, preheat a broiler (griller). Arrange the bread slices on a broiling pan and broil (grill), watching carefully to prevent burning, until golden, about 1½–2 minutes. Sprinkle each slice of bread with an equal amount of the Gruyère cheese and broil until the cheese melts, 1–2 minutes longer.

4. To serve, ladle into individual bowls and float 3 Gruyère croutons on top of each. Sprinkle an equal amount of parsley over each bowl.

Nutritional Analysis Per Serving:

CALORIES 377

(KILOJOULES 1,583)

PROTEIN 14 G

CARBOHYDRATES 50 G

TOTAL FAT 15 G

SATURATED FAT 4 G

CHOLESTEROL 16 MG

SODIUM 620 MG

DIETARY FIBER 5 G

A purée of roasted red bell pepper, vibrant in both color and taste, enhances the flavor and presentation of this satisfying yet light blend. If you wish, top with a sprinkle of grated Parmesan cheese and accompany with toasted baguette slices.

ROASTED EGGPLANT & GARLIC SOUP

Serves 4

2 red bell peppers (capsicums)
1 eggplant (aubergine), halved lengthwise
¼ teaspoon salt
⅛ teaspoon freshly ground pepper
3 garlic cloves, peeled
⅛ teaspoon cayenne pepper
1 tablespoon olive oil
1 yellow onion, finely chopped
4 cups (32 fl oz/1 l) Poultry Stock *(recipe on page 127)*
4 tablespoons (2 oz/60 g) coarsely chopped fresh basil

Nutritional Analysis Per Serving:

CALORIES 122
(KILOJOULES 513)
PROTEIN 4 G
CARBOHYDRATES 17 G
TOTAL FAT 5 G
SATURATED FAT 1 G
CHOLESTEROL 0 MG
SODIUM 189 MG
DIETARY FIBER 3 G

1. Preheat a broiler (griller). Place the bell peppers on a broiling pan under the broiler about 4 inches (10 cm) from the heat source. Roast, turning occasionally, until the skin is blistered and slightly charred on all sides, 6–8 minutes. Transfer to a brown paper bag, close it tightly and let rest for 10 minutes. Remove from the bag and peel off the charred skin. Halve the peppers and remove the stems, seeds and ribs.

2. Preheat an oven to 400°F (200°C). Coat a roasting pan with nonstick cooking spray. Sprinkle the eggplant halves with the salt and pepper. Place them, cut side up, and the garlic in the pan and bake, turning once, until brown and tender when pierced with a fork, about 45 minutes.

3. Halve the eggplant again and place in a food processor fitted with the metal blade. Add the garlic and purée, scraping down the sides of the bowl as necessary, until smooth but with a little texture remaining, about 20 seconds. Transfer to a bowl and set aside.

4. Wipe the processor bowl clean and add the bell peppers and cayenne pepper. Purée, scraping down the sides half-way through, until very smooth, about 1 minute.

5. In a saucepan over medium-low heat, warm the olive oil. Add the onion and sauté, stirring, until very tender, 10–12 minutes. Cover and cook for 5 minutes longer. Add the eggplant purée and Poultry Stock, stir to mix well and bring to a simmer. Stir until well blended.

6. To serve, ladle into individual bowls. Stir an equal amount of the red pepper purée into each serving, without mixing it in completely. Sprinkle 1 tablespoon basil atop each bowl.

Shallots, chives and angel hair pasta update this easy version of chicken soup with noodles. If you have no leftover chicken, poach 1 skinned and boned chicken breast in lightly salted water for about 12 minutes, then drain, cool and dice.

CHICKEN & VEGETABLE CAPELLINI SOUP

Serves 4

6 cups (48 fl oz/1.5 l) Poultry Stock
  (recipe on page 127)
1 leek, green and white parts,
  thinly sliced
2 carrots, peeled, halved lengthwise
  and thinly sliced crosswise
2 celery stalks, thinly sliced
1 tablespoon finely chopped
  fresh parsley
2 oz (60 g) dried capellini noodles
½ cup (3 oz/90 g) diced cooked
  chicken
salt and freshly ground pepper
1 tablespoon minced fresh chives

1. In a saucepan over medium-high heat, bring the Poultry Stock to a simmer. Add the leek, carrots, celery and parsley. Simmer, uncovered, until the vegetables are soft, about 15 minutes.
2. Add the noodles, lower the heat to medium and cook until al dente, 3–4 minutes, or according to package directions. Two minutes before the noodles are done, add the chicken and salt and pepper to taste. Stir to mix well and heat through.
3. To serve, ladle into individual bowls. Sprinkle each serving with an equal amount of the chives.

Nutritional Analysis Per Serving:

CALORIES 172
(KILOJOULES 722)
PROTEIN 11 G
CARBOHYDRATES 23 G
TOTAL FAT 4 G
SATURATED FAT 1 G
CHOLESTEROL 18 MG
SODIUM 122 MG
DIETARY FIBER 3 G

The sweet flavor of vitamin-rich carrots finds a natural complement in the lively spice of ginger. A splash of fresh orange juice only heightens the flavors and the vibrant color of this light, refreshing soup. Make it with vegetable stock, if you wish.

CARROT & GINGER SOUP

Serves 4

2 tablespoons canola oil or other vegetable oil

2 leeks, white part only, thinly sliced

1 lb (500 g) carrots, about 6, peeled and thinly sliced

1 large red potato, about ½ lb (250 g), peeled and coarsely diced

2 teaspoons minced fresh ginger

4 cups (32 fl oz/1 l) Poultry Stock *(recipe on page 127)*

½ cup (4 fl oz/125 ml) fresh orange juice

1 teaspoon grated orange zest

¼ teaspoon ground cinnamon

¼ teaspoon white pepper

salt

fresh mint sprigs

1. In a saucepan over medium heat, warm the oil. Add the leeks and sauté, stirring, until softened, about 2 minutes. Add the carrots, potato and ginger and sauté until the vegetables are just softened, 5–6 minutes.

2. Reduce the heat to medium-low, add the Poultry Stock and simmer, uncovered, until the vegetables are tender when pressed with a fork, about 25 minutes.

3. In a food processor fitted with the metal blade, process the soup for 15 seconds, in batches, leaving some texture. Add the orange juice, orange zest, cinnamon, pepper and salt to taste. Stir to mix well.

4. To serve, ladle into individual bowls. Garnish with the mint sprigs.

Nutritional Analysis Per Serving:

**CALORIES 226
(KILOJOULES 948)
PROTEIN 5 G
CARBOHYDRATES 34 G
TOTAL FAT 8 G
SATURATED FAT 1 G
CHOLESTEROL 0 MG
SODIUM 98 MG
DIETARY FIBER 5 G**

In place of the smoked ham that frequently flavors split pea soup, a garnish of crumbled crisp bacon contributes smoky flavor without too much fat or calories. But leave it out, if you like, and use vegetable stock for a vegetarian version.

Split Pea Soup

Serves 4

1 tablespoon olive oil
1 yellow onion, finely chopped
1 celery stalk, sliced
2 small carrots, peeled and sliced
¾ lb (375 g) fresh white mushrooms, sliced (4 cups)
1 cup (7 oz/220 g) split peas, picked over and rinsed
4 cups (32 fl oz/1 l) Poultry Stock *(recipe on page 127)*

2 tablespoons finely chopped fresh parsley
½ teaspoon finely chopped fresh marjoram or ¼ teaspoon dried marjoram
½ teaspoon finely chopped fresh thyme or ¼ teaspoon dried thyme
¼ lb (125 g) lean bacon
⅛ teaspoon salt
⅛ teaspoon freshly ground pepper
1 tablespoon fresh lemon juice

Nutritional Analysis Per Serving:

Calories 384
(Kilojoules 1,612)
Protein 24 g
Carbohydrates 45 g
Total Fat 13 g
Saturated Fat 3 g
Cholesterol 30 mg
Sodium 732 mg
Dietary Fiber 6 g

1. In a large saucepan over medium heat, warm the olive oil. Add the onion and sauté, stirring, until softened, 3–5 minutes. Add the celery, carrots and mushrooms and sauté, stirring, until just slightly softened, another 3 minutes.

2. Add the split peas, Poultry Stock, parsley, marjoram and thyme and bring to a simmer over medium-low heat. Cover partially and cook until the peas are tender, 50–60 minutes.

3. Meanwhile, in a frying pan over medium heat, fry the bacon until crisp, about 5 minutes. Using a slotted spatula, transfer to paper towels to drain.

4. Transfer 2 cups (16 fl oz/500 ml) of the soup to a food processor fitted with the metal blade or a blender and process until completely puréed. Return the puréed soup to the pan, add the salt, pepper and lemon juice and simmer gently for 5 minutes.

5. To serve, ladle into individual bowls. Crumble an equal amount of the bacon atop each bowl.

Chockful of vegetables and lean Canadian bacon, this soup is as robust as it is healthful. When white corn is in season, use it to give the soup an appealing garden-fresh sweetness. Feel free to substitute a milder green chili for the jalapeño.

SPICY CORN, RED PEPPER & POTATO CHOWDER

Serves 6

3 oz (90 g) Canadian bacon, sliced and cut into ½-inch (12-mm) dice

1 yellow onion, finely chopped

1½ lb (750 g) red or white rose potatoes, peeled and cut into ½-inch (12-mm) pieces

1 large red bell pepper, seeded, deribbed and cut into ½-inch (12-mm) dice

1 small fresh jalapeño pepper, seeded and minced

4 cups (32 fl oz/1 l) Poultry Stock *(recipe on page 127)*

½ teaspoon minced fresh thyme leaves or ¼ teaspoon dried thyme

3 cups (18 oz/560 g) corn kernels (from about 6 ears of corn)

⅓ cup (3 fl oz/80 ml) lowfat milk

½ teaspoon salt

⅛ teaspoon white pepper

1. Coat the bottom of a nonreactive stockpot with nonstick cooking spray and place over medium heat. Add the bacon and sauté, stirring, until crisp, about 5 minutes. Drain on a paper towel.

2. In the same pot over medium heat, add the onion and sauté, stirring, until softened but not browned, 3–5 minutes. Add the potatoes, reduce the heat to medium-low, and sauté, stirring, for 3 minutes longer. Add the bell pepper and jalapeño pepper and sauté, stirring, until the peppers are slightly wilted, 1 minute longer.

3. Add the Poultry Stock and thyme and bring to a boil. Reduce the heat to medium-low, cover partially and simmer until the potatoes are just tender, 20–25 minutes.

4. Ladle about one fourth of the potato mixture into a food processor fitted with the metal blade and process until puréed.

5. In the stockpot combine the purée, corn, milk, bacon, salt and pepper. Cook, uncovered, over medium-low heat for 5 minutes.

6. To serve, ladle into individual bowls.

Nutritional Analysis Per Serving:

CALORIES 207

(KILOJOULES 871)

PROTEIN 10 G

CARBOHYDRATES 38 G

TOTAL FAT 3 G

SATURATED FAT 1 G

CHOLESTEROL 8 MG

SODIUM 439 MG

DIETARY FIBER 5 G

Each region of Mexico seems to have its own variation on this soup, which makes clever use of stale tortillas to gain texture and flavor. Avocado is a traditional garnish, but leave it out if you wish to cut down on fat.

Tortilla Soup

Serves 4

1 tablespoon plus 1 teaspoon canola oil or other vegetable oil
1 small yellow onion, thinly sliced
2 garlic cloves, peeled
2 teaspoons chopped fresh cilantro (fresh coriander)
1 cup (6 oz/185 g) drained canned plum (Roma) tomatoes
4 cups (32 fl oz/1 l) Poultry Stock *(recipe on page 127)*
salt and freshly ground pepper

4 corn tortillas, preferably day-old, halved and cut into narrow strips
1 dried chili pepper, such as a pasilla pepper, stemmed, seeds forced out through the top and crumbled
2 green (spring) onions, green and white parts, thinly sliced
½ ripe avocado, halved, pitted, peeled and cut into ¼-inch (6-mm) cubes
4 tablespoons shredded jack cheese
2 teaspoons fresh lime juice

Nutritional Analysis Per Serving:

CALORIES 226
(KILOJOULES 951)
PROTEIN 7 G
CARBOHYDRATES 24 G
TOTAL FAT 13 G
SATURATED FAT 3 G
CHOLESTEROL 8 MG
SODIUM 228 MG
DIETARY FIBER 3 G

1. In a frying pan over medium-low heat, warm the 1 tablespoon of oil. Add the onion, whole garlic cloves and cilantro and sauté until the onion is golden brown, about 10 minutes.

2. In a food processor fitted with the metal blade, combine the onion mixture and tomatoes and process until smooth.

3. Heat the remaining 1 teaspoon oil in the same pan over medium-high heat and add the puréed tomato mixture. Cook, stirring frequently, until thickened and dark, 5–6 minutes. Transfer the mixture to a large saucepan and add the Poultry Stock. Cover partially and simmer over medium-low heat, stirring occasionally, until slightly thickened, 25–30 minutes. Add the salt and pepper to taste. Stir to mix well.

4. Preheat the oven to 400°F (200°C).

5. In a roasting pan, spread the tortilla strips and the dried chili evenly. Bake until crisp and beginning to brown, 7–8 minutes.

6. To serve, ladle into individual bowls. Garnish with an equal amount of the tortilla strips, green onions, avocado, chili, cheese and lime juice.

A swirl of fresh basil Pesto adds a burst of flavor, aroma and color to the classic Italian vegetable soup. Pastina is a tiny soup pasta available in Italian delicatessens and well-stocked food stores; if it is not available substitute orzo or other small pastas.

Minestrone with Pesto

Serves 6

1 tablespoon olive oil
1 large yellow onion, finely chopped
3 carrots, peeled and cut into ¼-inch (6-mm) dice
⅓ lb (155 g) red or white rose potatoes, peeled and cut into ¼-inch (6-mm) dice
1 zucchini (courgette), cut into ¼-inch (6-mm) dice
¼ small head green cabbage, shredded
½ cup (4 fl oz/125 ml) chopped tomatoes

6 cups (48 fl oz/1.5 l) Poultry Stock *(recipe on page 127)*
1 garlic clove, peeled and minced
¼ teaspoon ground oregano
½ teaspoon salt
¼ teaspoon pepper
½ cup (2 oz/60 g) pastina, uncooked
¾ cup (5 oz/155 g) canned white beans, rinsed and drained
¼ cup (2 fl oz/60 ml) Pesto *(recipe on page 125)*

1. In a large saucepan over medium heat, warm the olive oil. Add the onion and sauté, stirring occasionally, until beginning to soften but not color, 3–5 minutes. Add the carrots, potatoes and zucchini and sauté for 3 minutes longer. Add the cabbage and sauté just until softened, about 2 minutes more.

2. Add the tomatoes, Poultry Stock, garlic, oregano, salt and pepper and bring to a boil. Reduce the heat to medium-low and simmer, uncovered, until the vegetables are tender, about 25 minutes.

3. Meanwhile, fill a small saucepan three-fourths full of water and bring to a boil. Add the pastina and cook until al dente or according to package directions. Drain well, rinse in cool water and add to the soup. Add the white beans, stir to mix well and heat through.

4. To serve, ladle into individual bowls and top each serving with 2 teaspoons of the Pesto.

Nutritional Analysis Per Serving:

**Calories 222
(Kilojoules 934)
Protein 8 g
Carbohydrates 29 g
Total Fat 9 g
Saturated Fat 2 g
Cholesterol 11 mg
Sodium 395 mg
Dietary Fiber 5 g**

Bisques are typically rich with cream or butter. Here, lowfat buttermilk enriches without adding much fat. For the best flavor, use vine-ripened tomatoes. Although the soup is meant to be served chilled, it is good hot also.

Tomato & Buttermilk Bisque

Serves 6

2 tablespoons olive oil
2 leeks, green and white parts, finely chopped
1 carrot, peeled and finely chopped
1 celery stalk, finely chopped
4 ripe tomatoes, about 2 lb (1 kg) total weight, coarsely chopped
3 tablespoons tomato paste
2 tablespoons all-purpose (plain) flour
4 cups (32 fl oz/1 l) Poultry Stock *(recipe on page 127)*
2 tablespoons chopped fresh basil
salt and freshly ground pepper
¼ cup (2 fl oz/60 ml) lowfat buttermilk

1. In a saucepan, over low heat, warm the olive oil. Add the leeks, carrot and celery and sauté, stirring occasionally, until slightly softened, about 5 minutes.
2. Add the tomatoes and tomato paste and cook until the tomatoes start to soften, about 5 minutes longer. Sprinkle with the flour and stir to mix well. Add the Poultry Stock, cover and simmer until slightly thickened, about 20 minutes.
3. Stir in the basil and salt and pepper to taste, remembering that food served cold needs more seasoning. Transfer the soup to a food processor fitted with the metal blade and purée until smooth. Transfer to a nonreactive bowl. (For a velvety texture, using the back of a wooden spoon, press the purée through a sieve into the bowl.) Cover and refrigerate until well chilled.
4. To serve, transfer to individual bowls. Lightly stir in the buttermilk, leaving a visible swirl of it in the soup.

Nutritional Analysis Per Serving:

Calories 142
(Kilojoules 598)
Protein 4 g
Carbohydrates 20 g
Total Fat 6 g
Saturated Fat 1 g
Cholesterol 0 mg
Sodium 138 mg
Dietary Fiber 4 g

Mint adds a hint of sweet, cool flavor to an old-fashioned chicken soup. If you have no leftover chicken, poach 1 skinned and boned chicken breast in lightly salted water for about 12 minutes, then drain, cool and dice. Serve with hearty wheat bread.

CHICKEN & RICE SOUP

Serves 6

6 cups (48 fl oz/1.5 l) Poultry Stock
  (recipe on page 127)
½ white onion, finely chopped
2 carrots, peeled, halved lengthwise
  and thinly sliced
1 tomato, ½ lb (250 g) total weight,
  peeled and sliced
1 bay leaf

4 fresh mint sprigs
1 zucchini (courgette), halved lengthwise and thinly sliced
¼ cup (1½ oz/45 g) cooked white rice
½ cup (3 oz/90 g) shredded cooked
  chicken, left over from making
  the stock
salt and freshly ground pepper

1. In a saucepan over medium-high heat, bring the Poultry Stock to a simmer. Add the onion, carrots, tomato, bay leaf and mint sprigs. Simmer until the vegetables are soft, about 15 minutes.
2. Add the zucchini, rice and chicken and simmer until the zucchini is cooked and the rice and chicken are heated through.
3. Remove and discard the bay leaf and mint sprigs. Add the salt and pepper to taste. Stir to mix well.
4. To serve, ladle into individual bowls.

Nutritional Analysis Per Serving:

CALORIES 94
(KILOJOULES 395)
PROTEIN 7 G
CARBOHYDRATES 11 G
TOTAL FAT 2 G
SATURATED FAT 1 G
CHOLESTEROL 12 MG
SODIUM 71 MG
DIETARY FIBER 2 G

A Caribbean and Latin American favorite, black bean soup gains added color and zest—
and a good helping of Vitamin C—from a fresh, spicy salsa of grapefruit and orange.
For a vegetarian version, omit the ham hock or bone and use vegetable stock.

Black Bean Soup with Citrus Salsa

Serves 4

1 cup (7 oz/220 g) dried black
  beans, picked over and rinsed
1 tablespoon olive oil
1 yellow onion, finely chopped
2 garlic cloves, peeled and minced
½ teaspoon ground cumin
½ teaspoon ground coriander
5 cups (40 fl oz/1.25 l) Beef or
  Poultry Stock *(recipes on pages
  126–127)*
½ small ham hock or ham bone,
  about ¼ lb (125 g)
1 tablespoon fresh lime juice
¼ teaspoon salt
⅛ teaspoon freshly ground pepper
fresh cilantro (fresh coriander) sprigs

*Nutritional Analysis
Per Serving:*

Calories 284
(Kilojoules 1,191)
Protein 15 g
Carbohydrates 44 g
Total Fat 6 g
Saturated Fat 1 g
Cholesterol 8 mg
Sodium 405 mg
Dietary Fiber 8 g

Citrus Salsa
½ pink grapefruit
½ orange
1 small fresh jalapeño pepper, seeded
  and finely chopped
¼ small red (Spanish) onion, minced
2 tablespoons minced fresh chives
1 teaspoon sherry vinegar
⅛ teaspoon salt
⅛ teaspoon freshly ground pepper

1. Place the beans in a bowl with cold water to cover and
let stand for at least 4 hours or overnight. Alternatively, in
a saucepan, combine the beans with water to cover, bring
to a boil and boil for 2 minutes; remove from the heat,
cover and let stand for 1 hour. Drain the beans.
2. In a stockpot over medium-low heat, warm the olive oil.
Add the onion and sauté until the onions are translucent,
about 7 minutes. Add the garlic, cumin and coriander and
sauté for 3 minutes.
3. Add the beans, Beef or Poultry Stock and ham hock
or bone and bring to a boil. Reduce the heat to medium-
low, cover partially and simmer until the beans are soft,
1–1¼ hours. Remove and discard the hock or bone.
4. Prepare the Citrus Salsa (see opposite page).
5. In a food processor fitted with the metal blade, purée
the soup until smooth. Return to the pot and reheat.
Add the lime juice, salt and pepper.

6. To serve, ladle into individual bowls. Garnish each with 1 table-spoon of the Citrus Salsa and a cilantro sprig.

CITRUS SALSA

1. Peel the grapefruit and orange halves, removing all the white pith. Using a sharp knife, cut alongside the segments to release them from the membrane. Remove any seeds and chop the segments.
2. In a bowl, combine the grapefruit, orange, jalapeño pepper, onion, chives, sherry vinegar, salt and pepper. Stir to mix well.

The combination of fresh vegetables gives this soup an intense green color as well as a sweet flavor and satisfying texture—all of which become even more pleasing with the addition of a little lowfat sour cream and Pesto at serving time.

Lima Bean, Pea & Zucchini Purée with Pesto

Serves 4

2 tablespoons olive oil
2 small yellow onions, thinly sliced
4 zucchini (courgettes), thinly sliced
4 cups (32 fl oz/1 l) Poultry Stock
   (recipe on page 127)
2 cups (12 oz/375 g) fresh or frozen
   lima beans

1 cup (5 oz/155 g) fresh or
   frozen peas
¼ teaspoon salt
⅛ teaspoon freshly ground pepper
2 tablespoons lowfat sour cream
¼ cup (2 fl oz/60 ml) Pesto
   (recipe on page 125)

1. In a large saucepan over medium-high heat, warm the olive oil. Add the onions and zucchini and sauté, stirring often, until just turning golden, 6–7 minutes.

2. Add the Poultry Stock and bring to a boil. Add the lima beans and the peas. When the soup returns to a boil, reduce the heat to medium-low and simmer until the vegetables are soft, 20–25 minutes. Add the salt and pepper. Stir to mix well.

3. In a food processor fitted with the metal blade, purée the soup until completely smooth, 3–4 minutes. Transfer the soup to a clean pan and reheat gently to serving temperature.

4. To serve, stir the sour cream into the hot soup, then ladle into individual bowls. Spoon an equal amount of Pesto into each bowl.

Nutritional Analysis Per Serving:

CALORIES 338
(KILOJOULES 1,418)
PROTEIN 14 G
CARBOHYDRATES 36 G
TOTAL FAT 16 G
SATURATED FAT 3 G
CHOLESTEROL 4 MG
SODIUM 262 MG
DIETARY FIBER 5 G

Eastern Europe has given rise to many versions of the hearty peasant vegetable soup known as *borscht,* commonly served with dark rye bread. This recipe features vegetables alone, but, if you wish, you could add a smoked ham hock.

CHILLED BEET & CUCUMBER SOUP

Serves 8

2 lb (1 kg) beets (beetroots), trimmed (about 8 beets)

1 yellow onion, quartered

8 cups (64 fl oz/2 l) Poultry Stock *(recipe on page 127)*

1 cup (8 fl oz/250 ml) water

1 tablespoon sugar

2 cucumbers, peeled, seeded and cut into thin strips

2 tablespoons fresh lemon juice

2 tablespoons rice wine vinegar

½ teaspoon salt

¼ teaspoon freshly ground pepper

4 tablespoons (2 oz/60 g) finely chopped fresh dill

1 cup (8 oz/250 g) nonfat plain yogurt or lowfat sour cream

Nutritional Analysis Per Serving:

CALORIES 104

(KILOJOULES 437)

PROTEIN 5 G

CARBOHYDRATES 18 G

TOTAL FAT 1 G

SATURATED FAT 0 G

CHOLESTEROL 1 MG

SODIUM 265 MG

DIETARY FIBER 2 G

1. In a large, nonreactive stockpot over medium-high heat, combine the beets, onion, Poultry Stock, water and sugar. Cover and bring to a boil. Reduce the heat to low and simmer, covered, until the beets are tender, 45–60 minutes.

2. Using a slotted spoon, transfer the beets to a colander. Reserve the cooking liquid. Peel the beets under cold running water. Cut 3 beets in half. Cut the remaining beets into strips 1 inch (2.5 cm) long and ¼ inch (6 mm) wide. Cover and refrigerate.

3. Strain the cooking liquid through a fine-mesh sieve into a large bowl. Remove and discard the onion. In a food processor fitted with the metal blade, purée the 6 beet halves and 1 cup (8 fl oz/250 ml) of the strained liquid. Add to the remaining strained liquid in the bowl. Cover and refrigerate for at least 4 hours or overnight.

4. Add the beet strips, cucumber strips, lemon juice, rice wine vinegar, salt, pepper and half of the dill to the chilled beet mixture. Stir to mix well.

5. To serve, ladle into individual bowls and garnish with an equal amount of the yogurt or sour cream and the remaining dill.

SALADS

Crisp, leafy greens. Ripe red tomatoes. Juicy apples. Zesty grapefruit. Tender green beans. Crunchy winter vegetables. At every turn of the page, this chapter presents an opportunity to partake of vitamins, minerals, carbohydrates and fiber in the most delicious form nature has devised: fresh salads. No first course offers up a greater abundance of healthy garden produce than a salad, and the wide range of salads in this chapter engage the increasing variety of quality ingredients available in markets everywhere. But, in some of the recipes that follow, fruits and vegetables are only the beginning, providing a colorful, flavorful background for poached salmon, tuna, grilled chicken, sautéed scallops and other protein-rich offerings. Such salads make ideal first courses in menus with a vegetarian main dish featuring pasta, grains or beans. Others use grains, pasta or rice rather than greens as a base.

While designed as a first course, accompanied by some crusty bread these salads readily become a satisfying meal in their own right.

Poaching salmon in stock gives the rich-tasting fish even more flavor. If you don't have fish stock on hand, poach the salmon in water to which you have added a slice of lemon. A fresh herb dressing joins the fish and vegetables nicely.

COLD POACHED SALMON SALAD

Serves 4

2 cups (16 fl oz/500 ml) Fish Stock *(recipe on page 126)*

1 lb (500 g) salmon fillets

1 lb (500 g) thin asparagus, trimmed of tough ends

1 tablespoon capers, well rinsed and drained

3 tablespoons finely chopped fresh dill

2 tablespoons finely chopped fresh parsley

1 teaspoon finely chopped lemon zest

½ cup (4 fl oz/125 ml) Simple Vinaigrette *(recipe on page 124)*

½ cup (3 oz/90 g) corn kernels (from about 1 ear)

1 head red-leaf lettuce, torn into 2-inch (5-cm) pieces

12 cherry tomatoes, halved

Nutritional Analysis Per Serving:

**CALORIES 330
(KILOJOULES 1,386)
PROTEIN 27 G
CARBOHYDRATES 12 G
TOTAL FAT 20 G
SATURATED FAT 3 G
CHOLESTEROL 62 MG
SODIUM 252 MG
DIETARY FIBER 3 G**

1. In a deep frying pan or a large saucepan over medium heat, bring the Fish Stock to a simmer. The stock should be deep enough to cover the fish barely when it is added. Slip the fish into the stock and poach until opaque throughout when pierced with a knife, 10 minutes per inch (2.5 cm) at the thickest part. Remove the salmon and let cool. Remove the skin and bones and break up the salmon into 1½-inch (4-cm) pieces.

2. Fill a large frying pan three-fourths full of water and bring to a boil. Add the asparagus and cook until just tender, 3–5 minutes. Drain, let cool and cut into 2-inch (5-cm) lengths.

3. To make the dressing, in a food processor fitted with the metal blade, process the capers, dill, parsley, lemon zest and Simple Vinaigrette until creamy.

4. Combine the salmon, corn and asparagus in a mixing bowl. Drizzle on the dressing. Stir to mix well.

5. To serve, arrange the lettuce leaves on individual plates. Top with an equal amount of the salmon mixture and cherry tomato halves.

The wide choice of fresh greens in stores today makes it possible to turn a simple salad into a colorful, elegant first course to precede grilled seafood, poultry or meat. Sherry vinegar and olive oil yield a little dressing that goes a long way.

Three-Lettuce & Walnut Salad

Serves 4

½ head radicchio, torn into
   bite-sized pieces
1 small bunch arugula (rocket), torn
   into bite-sized pieces
1 small bunch limestone or
   butter lettuce
4 walnuts, shelled, toasted and
   chopped coarsely

1 tablespoon sherry vinegar
¼ teaspoon Dijon-style mustard
⅛ teaspoon salt
⅛ teaspoon freshly ground pepper
3 tablespoons olive oil

1. In a salad bowl, combine the radicchio, arugula and lime-stone or butter lettuce. Sprinkle the walnuts over the top.
2. To make the vinaigrette, in a small mixing bowl, whisk together the sherry vinegar, mustard, salt and pepper. Drizzle in the olive oil slowly, whisking constantly, until the dressing is well blended.
3. To serve, pour the dressing over the salad and toss well.

Nutritional Analysis Per Serving:

CALORIES 145
(KILOJOULES 611)
PROTEIN 2 G
CARBOHYDRATES 3 G
TOTAL FAT 15 G
SATURATED FAT 2 G
CHOLESTEROL 0 MG
SODIUM 89 MG
DIETARY FIBER 1 G

Long-grain white rice extends the costlier wild rice—which is, in fact, not rice at all but the nutty-tasting grain of an aquatic grass native to the American Midwest. Serve this salad before grilled chicken or meat, or as part of a buffet or picnic.

WILD RICE SALAD

Serves 4

⅓ cup (2 oz/60 g) wild rice
2 cups (16 fl oz/500 ml) water
½ teaspoon salt
⅓ cup (2½ oz/75 g) long-grain
   white rice
3 tablespoons fresh lime juice
¼ teaspoon salt
⅛ teaspoon fresh ground pepper

½ teaspoon finely chopped fresh chives
2 teaspoons finely chopped fresh parsley
2 tablespoons olive oil
1 carrot, peeled and cut into thin strips
   1 inch (2.5 cm) long and ⅛ inch
   (3 mm) wide
1 Valencia orange, peeled, seeded and
   cut into ¾-inch (2-cm) pieces
fresh parsley sprigs

*Nutritional Analysis
Per Serving:*

**CALORIES 191
(KILOJOULES 803)
PROTEIN 4 G
CARBOHYDRATES 29 G
TOTAL FAT 7 G
SATURATED FAT 1 G
CHOLESTEROL 0 MG
SODIUM 417 MG
DIETARY FIBER 2 G**

1. Place the wild rice in a sieve and rinse thoroughly with cold water. In a small saucepan, combine the wild rice, half of the water and half of the salt. Cover and bring to a simmer over medium heat. Reduce the heat to low and cook until the wild rice is tender, about 30 minutes. Drain and let cool completely.
2. In another small saucepan, combine the white rice, the remaining water and salt. Place over medium-high heat and bring to a boil. Cover, reduce the heat to very low and cook until all the water has been absorbed and the rice is tender, 20 minutes. Remove from the heat and let cool completely.
3. To make the vinaigrette, in a small mixing bowl, whisk together the lime juice, salt, pepper, chives and chopped parsley. Slowly add the olive oil, whisking constantly until well blended.
4. In a bowl, gently mix together the wild rice, white rice, carrot and orange pieces. Add the vinaigrette and toss to mix well. Cover and refrigerate 1–2 hours for the flavors to blend.
5. To serve, transfer to a serving bowl. Garnish with the fresh parsley sprigs.

Pasta healthfully extends the traditional ingredients of Italy's popular tricolor antipasto salad, relegating the cheese to a supporting rather than a featured role. For a more pungent flavor, substitute feta cheese, rinsed to reduce its saltiness.

Tomato, Basil & Mozzarella Pasta Salad

Serves 6

2 lb (1 kg) ripe plum (Roma) tomatoes, peeled, seeded and coarsely chopped

½ cup (¾ oz/20 g) coarsely chopped basil

⅓ cup (½ oz/15 g) finely chopped fresh flat-leaf (Italian) parsley

3 garlic cloves, peeled and minced

½ lb (250 g) lowfat mozzarella cheese, cut into ½-inch (12-mm) dice

¼ cup (1 oz/30 g) freshly grated Parmesan cheese

¼ teaspoon salt

⅛ teaspoon freshly ground pepper

½ cup (4 fl oz/125 ml) Simple Vinaigrette *(recipe on page 124)*

1 lb (500 g) dried linguine

whole basil leaves

1. In a serving bowl, combine the tomatoes, chopped basil, parsley, garlic, mozzarella and Parmesan cheeses, salt and pepper. Toss to combine. Add the Simple Vinaigrette and toss to mix well.

2. Fill a saucepan three-fourths full of water and bring to a boil. Add the linguine and boil until al dente or as directed on the package. Drain well.

3. To serve, add the pasta to the tomato-cheese mixture and toss well to distribute the ingredients evenly. Let cool to room temperature. Garnish with the basil leaves.

Nutritional Analysis Per Serving:

Calories 489
(Kilojoules 2,053)
Protein 22 g
Carbohydrates 67 g
Total Fat 15 g
Saturated Fat 5 g
Cholesterol 17 mg
Sodium 583 mg
Dietary Fiber 4 g

A wide selection of readily available cold-weather vegetables produces a fresh-tasting, crunchy salad that seems to announce spring's imminent arrival. You can vary the mixture by substituting feta or mozzarella cheese for the Gorgonzola.

CHOPPED WINTER VEGETABLE SALAD

Serves 6

1 fennel bulb, trimmed, cut into ¼-inch (6-mm) slices and then finely chopped

¼ small head white or green cabbage, cored and finely chopped

2 large tomatoes, seeded and finely chopped

6 radishes, finely chopped

½ cucumber, peeled, seeded and finely chopped

¼ jicama, peeled and finely chopped

2 carrots, peeled and finely chopped

1 celery stalk, finely chopped

¼ small red (Spanish) onion, finely chopped

½ cup (4 fl oz/125 ml) Balsamic Vinaigrette *(recipe on page 125)*

⅛ teaspoon salt

⅛ teaspoon freshly ground pepper

¼ cup (5 oz/155 g) crumbled Gorgonzola cheese

1½ tablespoons finely chopped mixed fresh herbs such as chives, basil and parsley

1. In a large mixing bowl, combine the fennel, cabbage, tomatoes, radishes, cucumber, jicama, carrots, celery and onion.

2. Pour the Balsamic Vinaigrette over the top. Add the salt and pepper and stir to mix well. Cover and refrigerate for at least 1 hour to blend the flavors.

3. To serve, mound the vegetable mixture in a serving bowl and sprinkle the cheese and the herbs over the top.

Nutritional Analysis Per Serving:

CALORIES 157
(KILOJOULES 660)
PROTEIN 4 G
CARBOHYDRATES 12 G
TOTAL FAT 11 G
SATURATED FAT 3 G
CHOLESTEROL 7 MG
SODIUM 334 MG
DIETARY FIBER 3 G

Serve this salad during warmer months as the quickly assembled first course of a backyard barbecue. Grilling the vegetables gives them a deliciously smoky flavor and complements their natural peak-of-season texture.

GRILLED CHICKEN & VEGETABLE SALAD

Serves 6

⅔ cup (5 fl oz/160 ml) Simple Vinaigrette *(recipe on page 124)*

1 teaspoon Dijon-style mustard

2 chicken breast halves, skinned and boned (8 oz/250 g total weight when boned)

8 asparagus, tough stem ends removed

3 small summer squash, cut lengthwise into slices ¼ inch (6 mm) thick

4 green (spring) onions, green and white parts

4 plum (Roma) tomatoes, halved lengthwise

2 ears corn, husks and silks removed

1 head romaine (cos) lettuce

1 small head napa cabbage, halved and core removed

⅛ teaspoon salt

2 tablespoons finely chopped mixed fresh herbs such as basil, parsley, dill and chives

Nutritional Analysis Per Serving:

CALORIES 218
(KILOJOULES 917)
PROTEIN 14 G
CARBOHYDRATES 17 G
TOTAL FAT 12 G
SATURATED FAT 2 G
CHOLESTEROL 22 MG
SODIUM 223 MG
DIETARY FIBER 5 G

1. In a small bowl, stir together the Simple Vinaigrette and mustard. Place the chicken breast halves in a small baking dish. Pour 2 tablespoons of the vinaigrette mixture evenly over the top. Let stand for 30 minutes, turning once or twice.

2. Meanwhile, prepare a fire in a charcoal grill. Away from the fire, coat the grill rack with nonstick cooking spray.

3. Place the asparagus, summer squash and green onions on the grill rack 3 inches (7.5 cm) from the fire and grill, turning once, until slightly charred, about 4 minutes on each side. Remove from the grill and chop into 1-inch (2.5-cm) pieces. Place in a serving bowl.

4. Place the tomato halves on the grill rack and grill, turning once, until charred but not mushy, 2–3 minutes. Remove from the grill and cut in half. Add to the bowl.

5. Place the corn on the rack and grill, turning as the kernels begin to darken, 3–4 minutes' total cooking time. Remove from the grill and, when cool enough to handle, cut off the corn kernels with a sharp knife. Add to the bowl.

6. Place the lettuce and cabbage on the grill rack and grill, turning to cook evenly, until the outsides are lightly charred, 3–5 minutes. Remove from the grill and chop coarsely. Add to the bowl.

7. Place the chicken on the grill rack. Grill, turning once and basting with the marinade, until no trace of pink remains when pierced with a knife, 5–7 minutes on each side. Remove from the grill and chop coarsely into 1-inch (2.5-cm) pieces. Add to the bowl.

8. To serve, add the salt and herbs and drizzle on the remaining vinaigrette mixture. Toss to mix well.

This popular Middle Eastern salad features fine bulgur, also known as cracked wheat, which requires only soaking in water to ready it for preparation. In place of the cilantro, try an equal quantity of fresh mint—a traditional seasoning for tabbouleh.

Confetti Vegetable Tabbouleh Salad

Serves 4

1 cup (6 oz/185 g) bulgur

1¾ cups (14 fl oz/440 ml) boiling water

⅓ cup (1½ oz/45 g) finely chopped red (Spanish) onion

⅓ cup (1½ oz/45 g) peeled, seeded and finely diced cucumber

⅓ cup (1½ oz/45 g) finely diced radishes

½ cup (3 oz/90 g) corn kernels (from about 1 ear), cooked

1½ tablespoons finely chopped fresh parsley

1½ tablespoons finely chopped fresh chives

2 tablespoons finely chopped fresh cilantro (fresh coriander)

1 tomato, seeded and diced into ½-inch (12-mm) pieces

½ cup (4 fl oz/125 ml) Simple Vinaigrette *(recipe on page 124)*

1 tablespoon fresh lemon juice

fresh cilantro (fresh coriander) leaves

1. Place the bulgur in a bowl and pour the boiling water over the top. Let stand for about 1 hour to allow the wheat to absorb the water.

2. Pour the bulgur into a colander to drain off any excess water. Place the bulgur in a dry kitchen towel and wring out any excess water. Place the bulgur in a dry bowl.

3. Add the red onion, cucumber, radishes and corn. Mix with a two-pronged fork so that the wheat stays fluffy and is not crushed. Add the parsley, chives, cilantro and tomato. Stir to mix well.

4. In a small bowl, whisk together the Simple Vinaigrette and lemon juice.

5. To serve, pour the vinaigrette mixture over the bulgur mixture and mix again with a two-pronged fork. Transfer to a serving bowl and garnish with the cilantro leaves.

Nutritional Analysis Per Serving:

CALORIES 267
(KILOJOULES 1,120)
PROTEIN 6 G
CARBOHYDRATES 36 G
TOTAL FAT 13 G
SATURATED FAT 2 G
CHOLESTEROL 0 MG
SODIUM 134 MG
DIETARY FIBER 8 G

The popular first course salad becomes all the more substantial with the addition of grilled chicken breast. The dressing has been lightened without reducing its familiar rich flavor. Toasting the croutons in the oven also reduces the overall fat.

CHICKEN CAESAR SALAD

Serves 6

12 thin slices French or sourdough bread, each ¼ inch (6 mm) thick and about 3 inches (7.5 cm) in diameter
4 tablespoons (1 oz/30 g) freshly grated Parmesan cheese
1 tablespoon fresh lemon juice
1 teaspoon olive oil
½ teaspoon Dijon-style mustard
⅛ teaspoon salt
⅛ teaspoon freshly ground pepper

2 chicken breast halves, boned and skinned (8 oz/250 g total weight when boned)
1 head romaine (cos) lettuce, torn into bite-sized pieces

CAESAR DRESSING
1 large egg
2 garlic cloves, peeled
2 tablespoons fresh lemon juice
½ teaspoon anchovy paste
⅛ teaspoon freshly ground pepper
¼ cup (2 fl oz/60 ml) olive oil
2 tablespoons freshly grated Parmesan cheese

Nutritional Analysis Per Serving:

CALORIES 245
(KILOJOULES 1,030)
PROTEIN 16 G
CARBOHYDRATES 14 G
TOTAL FAT 14 G
SATURATED FAT 3 G
CHOLESTEROL 62 MG
SODIUM 360 MG
DIETARY FIBER 2 G

1. To make the croutons, preheat an oven to 375°F (190°C). Place the bread slices in a single layer on a baking sheet. Using half of the Parmesan cheese, press an equal amount onto each bread slice. Toast until firm and slightly crisp, 10–12 minutes. Remove from the oven and let cool. Break into bite-sized pieces.
2. To prepare the chicken, preheat a broiler (griller). In a small bowl, stir together the lemon juice, olive oil, mustard, salt and pepper. Brush on the chicken. Broil (grill), turning once, until no trace of pink remains when pierced with a knife, 5–7 minutes. Slice on the diagonal into strips ¼ inch (6 mm) wide.
3. Prepare the Caesar Dressing (see opposite page).
4. To serve, in a serving bowl, combine the lettuce, the remaining Parmesan cheese, chicken strips and croutons. Drizzle the Caesar Dressing over the salad and toss well.

CAESAR DRESSING

1. Fill a small saucepan three-fourths full of water and bring to a boil. Carefully immerse the egg in the boiling water and immediately remove the pan from the heat. Cover and let stand for 10 minutes. Remove the egg from the water and let cool for 10 minutes.

2. In a food processor fitted with the metal blade, place the garlic and process to mince. Add the lemon juice, anchovy paste and pepper and process to combine. Add the olive oil in a fine, steady stream and pulse until emulsified.

3. Add the egg and pulse until combined, scraping down the sides of the work bowl as necessary. Add the Parmesan cheese and process until thoroughly blended and smooth.

This makes a wonderful first course for an elegant dinner party. If you can't find bay scallops, substitute larger sea scallops—but cut them into pieces no larger than 1 inch (2.5 cm). Peeled and deveined shrimp may also be used, if you prefer.

Warm Scallop Salad

Serves 6

¼ cup (2 fl oz/60 ml) plus
   1 tablespoon olive oil
2 shallots, finely chopped
2 tablespoons fresh lime juice
¾ teaspoon salt
½ teaspoon coarsely ground pepper
2 tomatoes, peeled, seeded, and
   chopped
2 tablespoons finely chopped
   fresh basil
1 lb (500 g) bay scallops
1 head Belgian endive (chicory/
   witloof)
1 bunch arugula (rocket), stems
   removed (about 2 cups/2 oz/60 g
   loosely packed)

*Nutritional Analysis
Per Serving:*

1. To make the dressing, in a frying pan over medium heat, warm the ¼ cup (2 fl oz/60 ml) olive oil. Add the shallots and sauté until soft, about 2 minutes. Stir in the lime juice, ½ teaspoon of the salt and the pepper. Remove from the heat and stir in the tomatoes and basil.

2. To prepare the scallops, in a nonstick frying pan over medium heat, warm the 1 tablespoon olive oil. Add the scallops and sauté, turning often, until translucent in the center when pierced with a knife, 3–5 minutes. Using a slotted spoon, transfer the scallops to a bowl. Add half of the dressing and the remaining ¼ teaspoon salt. Toss to mix well.

3. Cut off the core from the endive and separate the leaves. Cut each leaf lengthwise into quarters. Combine in a bowl with the arugula leaves and toss until mixed.

4. To serve, divide the greens evenly among individual plates. Spoon an equal amount of the warm scallops into the center of each plate. Spoon the remaining dressing around the scallops.

Calories 182
(Kilojoules 764)
Protein 13 g
Carbohydrates 5 g
Total Fat 12 g
Saturated Fat 2 g
Cholesterol 25 mg
Sodium 405 mg
Dietary Fiber 1 g

This salad's vivid palette of colors is almost as exciting as its combination of flavors and textures. Though avocado is featured, only half of one is portioned out over two servings—a judicious use of this rich, flavorful ingredient.

GRAPEFRUIT, AVOCADO & BEET SALAD

Serves 2

1 beet (beetroot), trimmed
½ large pink grapefruit
1 head red-leaf lettuce, cleaned and
  torn into bite-sized pieces

½ ripe avocado
¼ cup (2 fl oz/60 ml) Creamy Yogurt
  Dressing *(recipe on page 124)*
½ teaspoon honey

1. Fill a saucepan three-fourths full of water and bring to a boil. Add the beet and cook until tender but slightly resistant when pierced with a fork, 45–60 minutes. Drain. Peel under cold running water. Quarter the beet lengthwise, then cut each quarter into slices ¼ inch (6 mm) thick.
2. Peel the grapefruit half, removing all the white pith. Using a sharp knife, cut alongside the segments to release them from the membrane. Remove any seeds and halve crosswise.
3. In a large, shallow salad bowl, arrange the lettuce, sliced beets and grapefruit sections.
4. Pit the avocado half, if necessary, and peel it. Cut into ¼-inch (6-mm) cubes. Mound in the center of the bowl. Cover and refrigerate for up to 1 hour.
5. In a small bowl, whisk together the Creamy Yogurt Dressing and honey until well blended.
6. To serve, pour the dressing mixture over the salad.

Nutritional Analysis Per Serving:

**CALORIES 224
(KILOJOULES 942)
PROTEIN 4 G
CARBOHYDRATES 26 G
TOTAL FAT 14 G
SATURATED FAT 2 G
CHOLESTEROL 0 MG
SODIUM 225 MG
DIETARY FIBER 3 G**

Unlike dried beans, lentils require no presoaking, so they can be readily used for a last-minute salad. Tossing them while still warm with their tangy dressing helps them to absorb it. To reduce fat, soften the vegetables in a nonstick pan.

GREEN ONION, CARROT & LENTIL SALAD

Serves 4

1 cup (7 oz/220 g) dried lentils
2 cups (16 fl oz/500 ml) water
4 teaspoons olive oil
1 celery stalk, cut into ⅛-inch (3-mm) dice
1 carrot, peeled and cut into ⅛-inch (3-mm) dice
2 tablespoons red wine vinegar
1 tablespoon fresh lemon juice

1 tablespoon finely chopped fresh chives
1 tablespoon finely chopped fresh parsley
3 green (spring) onions, green and white parts, finely chopped
¼ teaspoon salt
⅛ teaspoon pepper
½ cup (2 oz/60 g) diced lowfat mozzarella
½ head red-leaf lettuce, torn into bite-sized pieces

Nutritional Analysis Per Serving:

CALORIES 253
(KILOJOULES 1,062)
PROTEIN 18 G
CARBOHYDRATES 33 G
TOTAL FAT 7 G
SATURATED FAT 2 G
CHOLESTEROL 5 MG
SODIUM 280 MG
DIETARY FIBER 7 G

1. In a saucepan, combine the lentils and water and bring to a boil. Reduce the heat to medium-low, cover partially and simmer until the lentils are tender but not mushy, 15–20 minutes. Remove from the heat, drain well and place in a bowl.

2. In a nonstick frying pan over medium heat, warm half of the olive oil. Add the celery and carrot and sauté until softened slightly, about 5 minutes. Transfer to the bowl holding the lentils.

3. Add the remaining olive oil, vinegar, lemon juice, chives, parsley, green onions, salt, pepper and cheese to the warm lentils and sautéed vegetables. Toss to mix well.

4. To serve, arrange one fourth of the lettuce on each plate. Mound an equal amount of the lentil mixture atop the lettuce.

A variation on Japan's widespread *sunomono* salad, this simple mixture of marinated cucumbers and toasted sesame seeds is ideal served just before or as an accompaniment to teriyaki chicken breasts or simply steamed seafood.

ASIAN CUCUMBER SALAD

Serves 4

2 teaspoons sesame seeds
2 teaspoons low sodium soy sauce
1 tablespoon rice wine vinegar
2 teaspoons sugar
2 teaspoons dark sesame oil

2 cucumbers, peeled, halved lengthwise, seeds removed and sliced cross-wise into slices ¼ inch (6 mm) thick
1 green (spring) onion, green and white parts, thinly sliced

1. In a frying pan over medium heat, shaking the pan occasionally, toast the sesame seeds until golden, 1–2 minutes. Watch carefully so the seeds do not burn.

2. In a serving bowl, whisk together the soy sauce, rice wine vinegar, sugar and sesame oil, mixing well to dissolve the sugar. Add the cucumbers and mix well to combine. Cover and refrigerate until slightly chilled.

3. To serve, stir the green onion and the sesame seeds into the serving bowl.

Nutritional Analysis Per Serving:

CALORIES 55
(KILOJOULES 233)
PROTEIN 1 G
CARBOHYDRATES 7 G
TOTAL FAT 3 G
SATURATED FAT 0 G
CHOLESTEROL 0 MG
SODIUM 110 MG
DIETARY FIBER 1 G

Although just a few ingredients go into this healthy variation on the classic French *céleri rémoulade,* it is nonetheless flavorful. Be sure to use a good-quality Dijon-style mustard—essential to capturing the salad's authentic flavor.

SHREDDED CARROT & CELERIAC SALAD

Serves 4

¾ lb (375 g) carrots (about 3 large), peeled and coarsely grated
1 lb (500 g) celeriac, peeled and coarsely grated
2 green (spring) onions, green and white parts, finely chopped

½ cup (4 fl oz/125 ml) Simple Vinaigrette *(recipe on page 124)*
½ teaspoon Dijon-style mustard
1 tablespoon finely chopped fresh parsley

1. In a serving bowl, combine the carrots, celeriac and green onions. Toss to mix well.
2. In a small bowl, whisk together the Simple Vinaigrette, mustard and parsley.
3. To serve, add the vinaigrette mixture to the vegetable mixture and toss to mix well.

Nutritional Analysis Per Serving:

CALORIES 185
(KILOJOULES 775)
PROTEIN 2 G
CARBOHYDRATES 18 G
TOTAL FAT 13 G
SATURATED FAT 2 G
CHOLESTEROL 0 MG
SODIUM 260 MG
DIETARY FIBER 3 G

Curried chicken salads usually include mayonnaise-based dressings. In this version substitute a yogurt dressing, which is lower in fat and calories. Because its flavor diminishes rapidly after opening, use curry powder soon after purchase.

CURRIED CHICKEN SALAD

Serves 4

4 chicken breast halves, skinned and boned (1 lb/500 g total weight when boned)

½ cup (3 oz/90 g) seedless green grapes, halved

2 celery stalks, thinly sliced

2 tablespoons finely chopped fresh parsley

½ cup (4 fl oz/125 ml) Creamy Yogurt Dressing *(recipe on page 124)*

⅛ teaspoon curry powder

1 tablespoon fruit chutney

1 head butter lettuce, pale, cup-shaped inner leaves only, separated

1. Fill a medium frying pan with high sides three-fourths full with water and bring to a boil. Add the chicken and simmer for 10–12 minutes or until just tender and juices run clear when pierced with a knife. Cool the chicken in the liquid. Drain and cut into 1½-inch (4-cm) chunks.

2. In a large bowl, combine the chicken, grapes, celery and half of the parsley.

3. In a small bowl, whisk together the Creamy Yogurt Dressing, curry powder and chutney until completely mixed. Add to the chicken mixture and toss to mix well.

4. To serve, divide the lettuce cups evenly among individual plates. Spoon an equal amount of the chicken mixture into each cup. Garnish with the remaining parsley.

Nutritional Analysis Per Serving:

**CALORIES 214
(KILOJOULES 899)
PROTEIN 28 G
CARBOHYDRATES 10 G
TOTAL FAT 7 G
SATURATED FAT 1 G
CHOLESTEROL 66 MG
SODIUM 283 MG
DIETARY FIBER 1 G**

Setting this first course salad apart are crisp broccoli florets, sweet roasted garlic and a scattering of toasted almonds—all of which make a small amount of poached chicken breast go a long way. Serve it with a dinner roll, if you like.

CHICKEN & BROCCOLI SALAD

Serves 6

1 garlic head
2 chicken breast halves, skinned and boned (8 oz/250 g total weight when boned)
4 cups (8 oz/250 g) broccoli florets
2 tablespoons finely chopped green (spring) onions or chives
⅓ cup (3 fl oz/80 ml) Creamy Yogurt Dressing *(recipe on page 124)*
½ teaspoon finely chopped lemon zest
¼ teaspoon salt
⅛ teaspoon white pepper
¼ cup (1 oz/30 g) slivered almonds, toasted

Nutritional Analysis Per Serving:

CALORIES 136
(KILOJOULES 573)
PROTEIN 12 G
CARBOHYDRATES 8 G
TOTAL FAT 7 G
SATURATED FAT 1 G
CHOLESTEROL 22 MG
SODIUM 206 MG
DIETARY FIBER 2 G

1. Preheat an oven to 425°F (220°C).
2. Using a sharp knife, cut off the top quarter of the garlic head. Score gently around the middle of the head, cutting through a few layers of the papery skin. Pull off the loose skin, trying not to remove every shred (this will make it easier to remove the cooked cloves later). Wrap the head tightly in a square of aluminum foil and place on a baking sheet. Bake until the garlic is soft when pierced with a knife, 45–60 minutes. Remove from the oven and let cool. Using your fingers, squeeze the soft garlic pulp from the skins into a small bowl and mash with a fork.
3. Fill a medium frying pan with high sides three-fourths full with water and bring to a boil. Add the chicken and simmer until just tender, 10–12 minutes. Cool the chicken in the liquid. Drain and cut into 1½-inch (4-cm) chunks.
4. Fill a large saucepan three-fourths full of water and bring to a boil. Add the broccoli, reduce the heat to medium-low and simmer, uncovered, until tender but not soft, 7–10 minutes. Drain, immerse in cold water to stop the cooking and preserve the color, cool and drain again.
5. In a small bowl, combine the green onions or chives, Creamy Yogurt Dressing, garlic purée and lemon zest.
6. In a serving bowl, combine the green onion mixture, chicken, broccoli, salt and pepper and stir gently to combine. Cover and refrigerate for 2–8 hours.
7. To serve, add all but 2 tablespoons of the toasted almonds and mix gently just to incorporate. Garnish with the remaining almonds.

The zesty lemon flavor of the dressing makes this salad an excellent first course or side dish for saucy barbecued chicken or turkey burgers. For a more colorful presentation, combine half of a red and half of a yellow bell pepper.

Mushrooms, Bell Pepper & Green Bean Salad

Serves 4

1 lb (500 g) green beans, trimmed
1 yellow or red bell pepper (capsicum), seeded, deribbed and cut into long, narrow strips
¼ lb (125 g) button mushrooms, cut into thin, narrow slices

¼ cup (2 fl oz/60 ml) Simple Vinaigrette *(recipe on page 124)*
2 teaspoons fresh lemon juice
1 teaspoon minced fresh chives

1. Fill a saucepan three-fourths full of water and bring to a boil. Add the green beans and cook until tender but still slightly crisp to the bite, 5–7 minutes; the timing will depend upon their size. Drain, immerse in cold water to stop the cooking and preserve the color, cool, drain again and place in a medium bowl.
2. Add the pepper and mushrooms to the green beans and toss to mix well.
3. In a small bowl, whisk together the Simple Vinaigrette, lemon juice and chives until thoroughly combined.
4. Add the vinaigrette mixture to the vegetables and toss to mix well. Cover and refrigerate until ready to serve.
5. To serve, transfer to individual plates.

Nutritional Analysis Per Serving:

CALORIES 99
(KILOJOULES 415)
PROTEIN 3 G
CARBOHYDRATES 10 G
TOTAL FAT 6 G
SATURATED FAT 1 G
CHOLESTEROL 0 MG
SODIUM 65 MG
DIETARY FIBER 2 G

Provence's *salade Niçoise,* which always presents a fresh selection of summer produce, becomes all the healthier when you use water-packed tuna and a lighter dressing. Add cooked beets and raw or roasted bell peppers for additional flavor and nutrients.

Mediterranean Tuna Salad

Serves 4

½ lb (250 g) red potatoes (about 2 medium)

¼ lb (4 oz/125 g) young, tender green beans, trimmed and halved crosswise (⅓ cup)

12¼ oz (380 g) white tuna canned in water, drained

⅓ cup (1¼ oz/45 g) drained, pitted and chopped Niçoise or Kalamata olives

½ small red (Spanish) onion, thinly sliced (¾ cup/3 oz/90 g)

1 tablespoon capers, rinsed and drained

1 tablespoon finely chopped fresh chervil or basil

⅛ teaspoon freshly ground pepper

½ cup (4 fl oz/125 ml) Simple Vinaigrette *(recipe on page 124)*

1½ teaspoons Dijon-style mustard

1 small head romaine (cos) lettuce, torn into bite-sized pieces

8 cherry tomatoes, halved

Nutritional Analysis Per Serving:

Calories 313

(Kilojoules 1,316)

Protein 25 g

Carbohydrates 19 g

Total Fat 16 g

Saturated Fat 2 g

Cholesterol 33 mg

Sodium 653 mg

Dietary Fiber 4 g

1. Fill a saucepan three-fourths full of water and bring to a boil. Add the potatoes and cook, uncovered, until tender but slightly resistant when pierced with a fork, 20–30 minutes. Drain and let cool. When cool enough to handle, peel and cut into strips 2 inches (5 cm) long, ½ inch (12 mm) wide and ½ inch (12 mm) thick. Place in a large bowl.

2. Fill a saucepan three-fourths full of water and bring to a boil. Add the green beans and cook until tender but still slightly crisp to the bite, 5–7 minutes. Drain, immerse in cold water to stop the cooking and preserve the color, cool, drain again and place in the bowl with the potatoes.

3. Add the tuna, olives, red onion, capers, chervil or basil and pepper and stir to mix well.

4. In a small bowl, whisk together the Simple Vinaigrette and mustard until well blended.

5. To serve, place an equal amount of the lettuce onto individual plates. Divide the potato mixture and cherry tomatoes between the servings and drizzle on the vinaigrette mixture.

Spinach is often paired with bacon in the salad bowl. Canadian bacon, far leaner than the streaky variety, offers a lowfat alternative without compromising on flavor. If you like, toss in a few walnuts for added crunch.

APPLES, CANADIAN BACON & SPINACH SALAD

Serves 4

⅔ cup (5 oz/155 g) very coarsely chopped Canadian bacon

¼ cup (2 fl oz/60 ml) Simple Vinaigrette *(recipe on page 124)*

1 teaspoon sherry vinegar

2 teaspoons olive oil or safflower oil

½ lb (250 g) spinach, stems removed and well dried (6 cups)

½ pippin or granny smith apple, peeled, cored and coarsely chopped

4 walnuts, shelled, toasted and coarsely chopped, optional

1. Coat a frying pan with nonstick cooking spray and place over medium heat. Place the bacon in the pan and fry until crisp, about 5 minutes. Transfer to paper towels to drain.

2. In a small bowl, whisk together the Simple Vinaigrette, sherry vinegar and oil.

3. To serve, tear the spinach into bite-sized pieces and place in a serving bowl. Add the apple and walnuts, if using. Sprinkle the bacon over the top and drizzle on the vinaigrette mixture. Toss to mix well.

Nutritional Analysis Per Serving:

CALORIES 152
(KILOJOULES 639)
PROTEIN 9 G
CARBOHYDRATES 5 G
TOTAL FAT 11 G
SATURATED FAT 2 G
CHOLESTEROL 18 MG
SODIUM 590 MG
DIETARY FIBER 1 G

BASIC TERMS & TECHNIQUES

The following entries provide a reference source for this volume, offering definitions of essential or unusual ingredients and explanations of fundamental cooking techniques.

AVOCADOS

Because this popular fruit derives 86 percent of its calories from fat, justifying its old-fashioned nickname of "Indian butter," a little avocado goes a long way as a garnish in first courses. The finest-flavored variety is the Hass, which has a pearlike shape and a thick, bumpy, dark green skin. Ripe, ready-to-use avocados will yield slightly to fingertip pressure.

To Remove the Pit: Using a sharp knife, cut down to the pit lengthwise all around the avocado. Gently twist the halves in opposite directions to separate; lift away the half without the pit.

Cup the half with the pit in the palm of one hand, with your fingers and thumb safely clear. Hold a sturdy, sharp knife with the other hand and strike the pit with the blade of the knife, wedging the blade firmly into the pit. Then twist and lift the knife to remove the pit.

BEANS AND LENTILS

Beans and lentils provide an important source of protein, fiber and complex carbohydrates and are good sources of essential B vitamins and minerals. Before use, dried beans and lentils should be carefully picked over to remove any impurities such as small stones or fibers or any discolored or misshapen beans. To rehydrate them, shorten their cooking time and improve their digestibility, presoak dried beans in cold water to cover generously for a few hours; lentils require nothing more than a quick rinsing. Rinse canned beans with water to flush out excess sodium.

Dozens of different kinds of beans are used in cuisines worldwide; some of the more common varieties, used in this volume, include:

BLACK BEANS These earthy-tasting, mealy-textured beans are relatively small in size with deep black skins. Also called turtle beans.

CANNELLINI BEANS Italian variety of small, white, thin-skinned, oval beans. Great Northern or white (navy) beans may be substituted.

GREAT NORTHERN BEANS Small to medium-sized white oval beans. White (navy) beans or cannellini may be substituted.

LIMA BEANS Flat, white, kidney-shaped beans with a mild flavor and soft texture. Larger dried lima beans may be substituted. Lima beans are also available fresh in season, as well as frozen.

WHITE (NAVY) BEANS Small, white, thin-skinned, oval beans. Also known as Boston beans. Great Northern beans may be substituted.

BEETS

These ruby-red root vegetables are good sources of potassium and other minerals. Because the color of beets bleeds easily into cooking liquids, always cook them before peeling, simmering them completely covered with water until tender when pierced with a fork, 45–60 minutes for medium-sized beets. Drain and rinse under cold running water until the beets are cool enough to handle; their skins will slip or peel off easily with a small, sharp knife.

CARROTS

This popular root vegetable, eaten raw or cooked, is an excellent source of vitamin A and beta-carotene, an antioxidant thought to play a role in preventing cancer. For the best texture, flavor and nutritional value, buy and cook them fresh. Smaller carrots generally have better flavor and texture; larger specimens tend to be woodier in texture and have a blander taste.

CITRUS FRUITS

The lively flavor of citrus fruits add fresh spark to healthy first courses. A touch of citrus zest is often a good alternative to added salt and the flesh of citrus fruit contains remarkable amounts of vitamin C.

To Section Citrus Fruit: Some recipes call for sections, or segments, of citrus fruit, free of pith and membranes. Using a small, sharp knife cut a thick slice off the bottom and top, exposing the fruit beneath the peel. Then, steadying the fruit on a work surface, thickly slice off the peel in strips, cutting off the white pith with it. Alternatively, hold the peeled fruit in one hand over a bowl to catch the juices. Using the same knife, carefully cut on each side of the membrane to free each section, letting the segment drop into the bowl as they are cut.

To Zest Citrus Fruit: The thin, brightly colored, outermost layer of a citrus fruit's peel, the zest, contains most of its aromatic essential oils—a lively source of flavor. Zest may be removed using one of two easy methods: Using a simple tool known as a zester, a fine hand-held shredder or grater, draw its sharp-edged holes across the fruit's skin to remove the zest in thin strips. Alternatively, holding the edge of a paring knife or vegetable peeler away from you and almost parallel to the fruit's skin, carefully cut off the zest in thin strips, taking care not to remove any white pith with it. Thinly slice or chop.

CORN

A good source of complex carbohydrates, protein and dietary fiber, as well as providing various vitamins and minerals, fresh sweet corn is one of the great pleasures of late summer and autumn. Before use, strip it of its green outer husks and the fine inner silky threads.

To Remove Kernels from an Ear of Corn: Hold the ear by its pointed end, steadying its stalk end on a cutting board. Use a sharp, sturdy knife to cut down and away from you along the ear, stripping off the kernels. Continue turning the ear with each cut.

CRUCIFEROUS VEGETABLES

This group of vegetables, named for their cross-shaped blossoms, includes broccoli, Brussels sprouts, cabbages, cauliflower, greens (collard, mustard and turnip), kale, kohlrabi, rutabagas

and turnips. They provide good sources of various vitamins and minerals and contain compounds that are thought to activate enzymes that destroy carcinogens.

To Cut Florets: Cut the flowerlike buds or clusters from the ends of the stalks, including about 1 inch (2.5 cm) of stem with each floret. Reserve the stalks for another use; they can, for example, be peeled of their tough, fibrous outer layers, then sliced and stir-fried or steamed until tender.

DAIRY PRODUCTS

The rich, mild flavor of milk and milk products can be incorporated into recipes with little or none of the fat present in whole milk, which contains 3.3 percent fluid fat and thus derives almost half of its calories from fat. Lowfat milk with 2 percent fluid fat, by contrast, gets only 35 percent of its calories from fat; lowfat milk with 1 percent fluid fat has only 23 percent fat calories; and nonfat milk typically derives only 5 percent of calories from fat. Similar percentages also apply to yogurt, which adds tangy enrichment much as sour cream would; seek out, too, the lowfat and nonfat sour creams now

being carried in food stores. Lowfat buttermilk, though it has a rich, tangy flavor and thick, creamy texture, has just 1.5 percent fluid fat, with only 20 percent of calories from fat. And, of course, all dairy products are a primary source of calcium as well as vitamins A and D.

GARLIC

The pungent bulb is popular worldwide as a flavoring ingredient, both raw and cooked. For the best flavor, purchase whole heads of dry garlic, separating individual cloves from the head as needed; it is best not to purchase more than you will use in 1 or 2 weeks, as garlic can shrivel and lose its flavor with prolonged storage.

To Peel a Garlic Clove: Place on a work surface and cover with the side of a large chef's knife. Press down firmly but carefully on the side of the knife to crush the clove slightly; the dry skin will then slip off easily.

HERBS

Many fresh and dried herbs enhance the flavor of healthy first courses without adding fat, calories or sodium. In general, add fresh herbs towards the end of cooking, as their flavor dissi-

pates with long exposure to heat; use dried herbs in dishes that cook longer. Measure for measure, dried herbs are twice as concentrated in flavor as their fresh counterparts.

To Chop Fresh Herbs: Wash the herbs under cold running water and thoroughly shake dry. If the herb has leaves attached along woody stems, strip the leaves from the stems; otherwise, as in the case of the parsley, hold the stems together. Gather up the leaves into a tight, compact bunch. Using a chef's knife, carefully cut across the bunch to chop the leaves coarsely. Discard the stems.

For more finely chopped herbs, gather the coarsely chopped leaves together. Steadying the top of the knife blade with one hand, rock the blade back and forth in an arc until the desired fineness is reached.

To Crush Dried Herbs: If using dried herbs, using your thumb, crush them in the palm of the hand to release their flavor. Alternatively, warm them in a frying pan and crush using a mortar and pestle.

LEEKS

These sweet, moderately flavored members of the onion family are long and cylindrical in shape, with a pale white root end and dark green leaves. Select firm, unblemished leeks, small to medium in size. Grown in sandy soil, the leafy-topped, multi-layered vegetables require thorough cleaning.

Trim off the tough ends of the dark green leaves. Trim off the roots. If a recipe calls for the white part, trim off the dark green leaves where they meet the slender pale-green part of the stem. Starting about 1 inch (2.5 cm) from the root end, slit the leek lengthwise.

Vigorously swish the leek in a basin or sink filled with cold water. Drain and rinse again; check to make sure that no dirt remains between the tightly packed pale portion of the leaves.

To Slice a Leek: Hold it steadily on a cutting surface and, using a sharp knife, cut crosswise starting at the root end. If a recipe calls for chopped leek, simply chop the slices.

NUTS

Although nuts are high in fat and should be avoided in large quantities in a health-conscious diet, they can nevertheless be added to recipes in small quantities to contribute their characteristic flavor and texture—as well as many difficult-to-get vitamins and minerals—with just a little added fat. Finely ground nuts prepared at home from unsalted shelled nuts allow this to be accomplished easily.

To Toast Nuts: Toasting brings out the full flavor and aroma of nuts. To toast any kind of nut, preheat an oven to 325°F (165°C). Spread the nuts in a single layer on a baking sheet and toast in the oven until they just begin to change color, 5–10 minutes. Remove from the oven and let cool to room temperature. Alternatively, a small quantity of nuts may be toasted in a single layer in a dry heavy frying pan over low heat, stirring frequently to prevent scorching.

Toasting also loosens the skins of nuts such as hazelnuts and walnuts, which may be removed by wrapping the still-warm nuts in a cotton towel and rubbing against them with the palms of your hands.

To Chop Nuts: Spread them in a single layer on a nonslip cutting surface. Using a chef's knife, carefully chop the nuts with a gentle rocking motion. Alternatively, put a handful or two of nuts in a food processor fitted with the metal blade and use a few rapid on-off pulses to chop the nuts to desired consistency; repeat with the remaining nuts. Be careful not to process the nuts too long or their oils will be released and the nuts will turn into a paste.

OILS

Oils provide both a medium in which foods may be browned without sticking, and also subtly enhance the flavor of recipes in which they are used—particulary when part of a salad dressing. Although oil is nothing more than a vegetable fat that is liquid at room temperature, and therefore derives 100 percent of its calories from fat, a relatively small amount of oil can nonetheless aid cooking and add distinctive flavor. Oils are also an excellent source of vitamin E and play an essential role in transporting the fat-soluble vitamins in our diet. Vegetable oils contain no cholesterol. Store all oils in tightly covered containers in a cool, dark place.

Extra-virgin olive oil, extracted from olives on the first pressing without use of heat or chemicals, is prized for its pure, fruity taste and golden to pale green hue. To get the most flavor from extra-virgin olive oil, use it uncooked in dressings and marinades. Products labeled pure olive oil, or simply olive oil, are blends from various pressings and may be used for all-purpose cooking.

Rich, flavorful and aromatic sesame oil is pressed from sesame seeds. Sesame oils from China and Japan are made with toasted sesame seeds, resulting in a dark, strong oil used as a flavoring ingredient; their low smoking temperature makes them unsuitable for using alone for cooking. Cold-pressed sesame oil, made from untoasted seeds, is lighter in color and taste and may be used for cooking.

Flavorless vegetable and seed oils such as safflower, corn and canola (rapeseed) oil are employed for their high cooking temperatures and bland flavor.

ONIONS

All manner of onions are used to enhance the flavor of healthy first courses and are a good source of minerals in the diet. Green onions, also called spring onions or scallions, are a variety harvested immature, leaves and all, before their bulbs have formed. The green and white parts may both be enjoyed, raw or cooked, for their mild but still pronounced onion flavor. Red (Spanish) onions are a mild, sweet variety of onion with purplish-red skin and red-tinged white flesh. White-skinned, white-fleshed onions tend to be sweet and mild. Yellow onions are the common, white-fleshed, strong-flavored variety distinguished by their dry, yellowish-brown skins.

PASTA

The growing popularity of pasta as a healthy staple rich in complex carbohydrates and proteins has resulted in an ever widening range of pasta choices available in food stores and specialty shops. Home cooks can choose from both fresh and dried pastas, made with or without eggs, and plain or flavored with a variety of vividly colored seasonings.

To Cook Pasta: To cook any pasta perfectly al dente—tender but still chewy—use enough boiling water to let the pasta circulate freely; adding salt to the water is not necessary. For 1 lb (500 g), you'll need about 5 qt (5 l) of water. Cooking time will depend on the pasta's shape, size and dryness, with fresh pasta generally taking 1–3 minutes and dried 3–15 minutes. Check suggested times on packaging, and test for doneness by removing a piece, letting it cool briefly and then tasting.

PEPPERS

The widely varied pepper family ranges in form and taste from large, mild bell peppers (capsicums) to tiny, spicy-hot chilies.

Fresh, sweet-fleshed bell peppers are most common in the unripe green form, although ripened red or yellow varieties are also available. Creamy pale yellow, orange and purple-black types may also be found. All bell peppers (capsicums) are a good source of vitamin C.

Red, ripe chilies are sold fresh and dried. Fresh green chilies include the mild-to-hot, dark green poblano, which resembles a tapered, triangular bell pepper; the long, mild Anaheim, or New Mexican; and the small, fiery serrano and jalapeño. When handling chilies, wear kitchen gloves to prevent any cuts or abrasions on your hands from contacting the peppers' volatile oils; wash your hands well with warm, soapy water and take special care not to touch your eyes or other sensitive areas.

To Seed Raw Peppers: Cut the pepper in half lengthwise with a sharp knife. Pull out the stem section from each half, along with the cluster of seeds attached to it. Alternatively, remove any remaining seeds, along with any thin white membranes, or ribs, to which they are attached.

RICE

Among the many varieties of rice grown, milled and cooked around the world, the most popular are long-grain white rices, whose slender grains steam to a light, fluffy consistency. Seek out some of the more fragrant, flavorful varieties such as basmati and jasmine rice. Follow package cook-

ing instructions. As a rule, however, allow 2 cups of water for every cup of uncooked rice. Bring the water to a boil and add the rice; when the water returns to a boil, reduce the heat to very low, cover and cook, without uncovering, until all the water has been absorbed and the rice is tender—usually about 20 minutes for long-grain white rice. Unpolished brown rice retains more fiber and nutrients, including B vitamins, than white rice. Because it still has the bran, brown rice needs to be cooked slightly longer and with more water than white rice. Wild rice, actually the seeds of a grass unrelated to conventional rice, is prized for its rich, nutlike flavor and chewy texture; it is also high in protein, carbohydrates, fiber and minerals.

SHELLFISH

Succulent and flavorful, fresh shellfish rank among the most popular of healthy first course ingredients, being high in protein and low in calories; though relatively high in sodium, they are generally included in sodium-restricted diets when no additional salt is used in their preparation or sauces.

All shellfish should be purchased only fresh and in season from a reputable merchant. They should be free of odor, giving off only a fresh clean scent

of the sea. Bivalves and mollusks such as clams, mussels and oysters should be alive, and their shells should close tightly when handled; avoid any that do not close, or those with shells that gape open. Use the following guidelines for the shellfish varieties used in this book:

CRAB MEAT Already-cooked crab meat is widely available in fish markets or at the seafood counters of quality food markets. Most often, it has been frozen; for best flavor and texture, seek out fresh crab meat. When fresh crab is in season, fish markets will usually sell crabs boiled or steamed whole; ask for them to be cracked, so that you can open the shells by hand and remove the meat. Left in coarse chunks, the shelled meat, particularly from the body of the crab, is known and sold as "lump" crab meat; finer particles of crab meat, from the legs or broken down from larger lumps, is known as "flaked" crab meat. Avoid imitation crab meat (surimi), which has inferior flavor and texture and is considerably higher in sodium.

MUSSELS Before cooking, the popular, bluish black-shelled bivalves require special cleaning to remove any dirt adhering to their shells and to remove their "beards," the fibrous threads by which the mussels connect to rocks or piers in the coastal waters where they live. Rinse the mussels thoroughly under cold running water. One at a time, hold them under the water and scrub with a firm-bristled brush to remove any stubborn dirt. Firmly grasp the fibrous beard attached to the side of each mussel and pull it off. Check all the mussels carefully, discarding those whose shells are not tightly closed.

SCALLOPS The bivalve mollusks, usually sold already shelled, come in two varieties: the round flesh of sea scallops is usually 1½ inches (4 cm) in diameter, while that of the bay scallop is considerably smaller.

SHRIMP Fresh, raw shrimp (prawns) are generally sold with the heads already removed but the shells still intact. Before cooking they are usually peeled and their thin, veinlike intestinal tracts removed. Using your thumbs, split open the thin shell along the concave side, between its two rows of legs. Peel away the shell, taking care to leave the last segment with tail fin intact and attached to the meat. Using a small, sharp knife, carefully make a shallow slit along the back, just deep enough to expose the long, usually dark, veinlike intestinal tract. With the tip of the knife or your fingers, lift up and pull out and discard the vein.

SPICES

A variety of dried spices—derived primarily from aromatic seeds, roots and barks—enhance the flavor of healthy first courses. As their flavor dissipates quickly, buy spices in relatively small quantities and store them in tightly covered containers in a cool, dark place. Some of the most common spices, used in this book, include:

CAYENNE PEPPER Very hot ground spice derived from dried cayenne chili peppers.

CORIANDER SEEDS Small, spicy-sweet seeds of the coriander plant, which is also called cilantro or Chinese parsley. Used whole or ground as a seasoning, particularly in Middle Eastern and Indian cuisines.

CUMIN Middle Eastern spice with a strong, dusky, aromatic flavor, popular in cuisines of its region of origin along with those of Latin America, India and parts of Europe. Sold either ground or as whole, small, crescent-shaped seeds.

CURRY POWDER Generic term for blends of spices commonly used to flavor East Indian–style dishes. Most curry powders will include coriander, cumin, chili powder, fenugreek and turmeric; other additions may include cardamom, cinnamon, cloves, allspice, fennel seeds and ginger. Best purchased in small quantities, because flavor diminishes rapidly after opening.

GINGER The rhizome of the tropical ginger plant, which yields a sweet, strong-flavored spice. Whole ginger rhizomes, commonly but mistakenly called roots, may be purchased fresh in a food store or vegetable market. Ground, dried ginger is easily found in jars or tins in the spice section.

PEPPER The most common of all savory spices is best purchased as whole peppercorns, to be ground in a pepper mill as needed, or coarsely crushed. Pungent black peppercorns derive from slightly underripe pepper berries, whose hulls oxidize as they dry. Milder white peppercorns come from fully ripened berries, with the husks removed before drying.

RED PEPPER FLAKES Coarsely ground flakes of dried red chilies, including seeds, which add moderately hot flavor to the foods they season.

SAFFRON Intensely aromatic spice, golden-orange in color, made from the dried stigmas of a species of crocus; used to perfume and color many classic Mediterranean and East Indian dishes. Sold as threads—the dried stigmas—or in powdered form. Look for products labeled pure saffron.

TOMATOES

Seek out fresh tomatoes with a deep red color that are firm to the touch and store them in a cool, dark place. Refrigeration causes tomatoes to break down quickly; use within a few days of purchase. All tomatoes are a good source of vitamin C. When good fresh tomatoes are not available, canned whole plum tomatoes are also good for cooking purposes. If you are following a reduced-sodium diet, seek out a brand that packages them without added salt.

VINEGARS

Literally "sour wine," vinegar results when certain strains of yeast cause wine—or some other alcoholic liquid such as apple cider, sherry or Japanese rice wine—to ferment for a second time, turning it acidic.

The best-quality wine vinegars begin with good-quality wine. Red wine vinegar, like the wine from which it is made, has a more robust flavor than vinegar produced from white wine. Balsamic vinegar, a specialty of Modena, Italy, is a vinegar made from reduced grape juice and aged for many years. Sherry vinegar has a rich flavor reminiscent of the wooden casks in which sherry is aged.

Basic recipes

The following basic recipes used throughout this volume provide fresh, preservative-free alternatives to similar commercial products.

Simple Vinaigrette

This recipe reduces the classic proportion of oil to vinegar, and the addition of boiling water helps to create a good emulsion while lightening the consistency. Feel free to add other favorite fresh herbs.

Makes about 1 cup (8 fl oz/250 ml)

1 shallot, finely chopped
1 garlic clove, peeled and minced
1 tablespoon finely chopped fresh parsley
1 teaspoon Dijon-style mustard
1 tablespoon fresh lemon juice
3 tablespoons red wine vinegar
⅓ cup (3 fl oz/80 ml) extra-virgin olive oil
3 tablespoons water, boiling
¼ teaspoon salt
⅛ teaspoon freshly ground pepper

1. In a bowl, combine the shallot, garlic, parsley, mustard, lemon juice and red wine vinegar and whisk to mix well. Alternatively, in a food processor fitted with the metal blade, combine the ingredients and process until well blended.
2. Slowly add the olive oil, whisking continuously until well blended. If using a food processor, with the motor running, slowly add the oil and process until blended. Add the boiling water, salt and pepper and whisk to mix well.

Per 1 Tablespoon Serving: Calories 55 (Kilojoules 232), Protein 0 g, Carbohydrates 1 g, Total Fat 6 g, Saturated Fat 1 g, Cholesterol 0 mg, Sodium 58 mg, Dietary Fiber 0 g

Creamy Yogurt Dressing

Nonfat plain yogurt gives this zesty vinaigrette a creamy consistency without adding any fat. Try whisking in a spoonful of honey with the vinegar and lemon juice to make a honey-mustard dressing.

Makes about 1 cup (8 fl oz/250 ml)

2 shallots, finely chopped
3 tablespoons red wine vinegar
4 teaspoons fresh lemon juice
2 teaspoons Dijon-style mustard
3 tablespoons extra-virgin olive oil
2 tablespoons water, boiling
¼ cup (2 oz/60 g) nonfat plain yogurt
½ teaspoon salt
⅛ teaspoon freshly ground pepper

1. In a small mixing bowl, combine the shallots, vinegar, lemon juice and mustard and whisk to mix well.
2. Slowly add the olive oil, whisking continuously until well blended. Add the boiling water, yogurt, salt and pepper and whisk to mix well.

Per 1 Tablespoon Serving: Calories 27 (Kilojoules 112), Protein 0 g, Carbohydrates 1 g, Total Fat 3 g, Saturated Fat 0 g, Cholesterol 0 mg, Sodium 90 mg, Dietary Fiber 0 g

BALSAMIC VINAIGRETTE

Balsamic vinegar, a specialty of Modena, Italy, contributes great character to this versatile dressing. For best results, select a good-quality aged balsamic vinegar with a well-balanced flavor— not too sweet and not too acidic.

Makes about ¾ cup (6 fl oz / 180 ml)

1 shallot, finely chopped
2 teaspoons Dijon-style mustard
¼ cup (2 fl oz / 60 ml) balsamic vinegar
⅓ cup (3 fl oz / 80 ml) extra-virgin olive oil
1 tablespoon fresh lemon juice
2 tablespoons water, boiling
¼ teaspoon salt
⅛ teaspoon freshly ground pepper

1. In a small bowl, combine the shallot, mustard and vinegar and whisk to mix well.
2. Slowly add the olive oil, lemon juice and water, whisking continuously until well blended. Add the salt and pepper and whisk to mix well.

Per 1 Tablespoon Serving: Calories 55 (Kilojoules 232), Protein 0 g, Carbohydrates 0 g, Total Fat 6 g, Saturated Fat 1 g, Cholesterol 0 mg, Sodium 71 mg, Dietary Fiber 0 g

PESTO

A specialty of Milan, pesto—which literally means "paste"—is traditionally a mixture of fresh basil, garlic, pine nuts, olive oil and Parmesan. This lowfat version eliminates the nuts and reduces the oil and cheese without diminishing the flavor.

Makes about ¾ cup (6 fl oz / 180 ml)

2 garlic cloves, peeled
1½ cups (1½ oz / 45 g) medium-packed fresh
  basil leaves (about 1 medium bunch)
1 cup (1 oz / 30 g) fresh parsley leaves
⅓ cup (3 fl oz / 80 ml) olive oil
¼ teaspoon freshly ground pepper
⅓ cup (1½ oz / 45 g) freshly grated
  Parmesan cheese

1. In a food processor fitted with the metal blade, process the garlic until puréed. Add the basil and parsley; process until finely chopped.
2. With the motor still running, slowly pour in the olive oil in a fine, steady stream, processing until thick. Add the pepper and cheese and process until well blended. Store in a tightly covered container in the refrigerator.

Per 1 Tablespoon Serving: Calories 74 (Kilojoules 310), Protein 2 g, Carbohydrates 2 g, Total Fat 7 g, Saturated Fat 1 g, Cholesterol 2 mg, Sodium 59 mg, Dietary Fiber 0 g

FISH STOCK

Keep this easy stock on hand to give outstanding flavor to your fish soups or chowders. For the best, most versatile results, use only a non-oily white fish such as halibut, snapper or rockfish.

Makes about 8 cups (64 fl oz / 2 l)

1 tablespoon vegetable oil
1 lb (500 g) fish heads (gills removed), skin, bones, flesh and trimmings
1 small yellow onion, thinly sliced
1 carrot, peeled, cut into 2-inch (5-cm) lengths
4 fresh parsley stems
1 celery stalk with leaves, cut into 2-inch (5-cm) lengths
1 bay leaf
5 white peppercorns
3 fresh dill sprigs
½ lemon, thinly sliced

1. In a 4-qt (4-l) stockpot over low heat, warm the vegetable oil. Add the fish parts and sauté for 2–3 minutes. Do not allow to brown.
2. Add the onion, carrot, parsley, celery, bay leaf, peppercorns, dill, lemon and water to almost cover. Bring to a boil over medium heat. Reduce the heat to low and simmer, uncovered, for 45 minutes.
3. Line a large sieve or a colander with cheesecloth (muslin) and strain the stock through it into a clean container. Using a large spoon, remove and discard the fat from the surface.
4. If not using immediately, pour the stock into tightly covered containers and refrigerate for up to 3 days or freeze for up to 2 months.

Per 1 Cup Serving: Calories 21 (Kilojoules 89), Protein 1 g, Carbohydrates 1 g, Total Fat 2 g, Saturated Fat 0 g, Cholesterol 0 mg, Sodium 261 mg, Dietary Fiber 0 g

BEEF STOCK

If thoroughly skimmed, this stock will add robust flavor without much fat. Depending upon the recipe in which you will use it, make the stock with beef for a richer, meaty flavor, or veal for lighter results.

Makes about 3½ qt (3.5 l)

2 lb (1 kg) veal necks and 1 lb (500 g) veal bones or 3 lb (1.5 kg) beef bones
1 fresh parsley stem
1 bay leaf
1 fresh thyme sprig
2 large carrots, unpeeled, cut into 2-inch (5-cm) lengths
1 large yellow onion, cut into slices 2 inches (5 cm) thick
2 leeks, green and white parts, cut into 2-inch (5-cm) lengths

1. Preheat an oven to 425°F (220°C).
2. Place the veal necks and bones or the beef bones in a large roasting pan. Roast until browned, about 1½ hours, turning every half hour.
3. Remove the roasting pan from the oven and place on top of the stove. Transfer the bones to a 6-qt (6-l) stockpot. Add about 3 cups (24 fl oz/ 750 ml) water to the roasting pan over medium-high heat. Bring the water to a boil, stirring and scraping up browned bits from the pan bottom. The water should become a rich brown color.
4. Pour the water from the roasting pan into the stockpot and add enough additional water to cover the bones. To make a bouquet garni, place the parsley stem, bay leaf and thyme sprig on a small square of cheesecloth (muslin), bring the corners together and tie securely with kitchen string. Add to the stockpot, along with the carrots, onion and leeks. Bring mixture to a boil over medium heat, then turn down the heat

as low as possible. Simmer, uncovered, for 8–10 hours or overnight, skimming occasionally.

5. Remove from the heat and let cool. Remove the bones and discard. Pour the stock through a fine-meshed sieve (a conical strainer is excellent for this purpose) into a large bowl. Let cool, cover and refrigerate until a layer of fat solidifies on top, about 2 hours. Using a large spoon, lift or spoon off the hardened fat and discard.

6. Line the sieve with cheesecloth (muslin) and pour the stock through it into a large clean bowl. The stock should be fat free and clear.

7. If not using immediately, pour the stock into tightly covered containers and refrigerate for up to 3 days or freeze for up to 2 months.

Per 1 Cup Serving: Calories 15 (Kilojoules 63), Protein 1 g, Carbohydrates 3 g, Total Fat 0 g, Saturated Fat 0 g, Cholesterol 0 mg, Sodium 7 mg, Dietary Fiber 0 g

POULTRY STOCK

This versatile stock contributes excellent flavor to soups and sauces. Store in a tightly covered container, in the refrigerator for up to 3 days or in the freezer for up to 2 months. For convenience, use 1-qt (1-l) or smaller containers.

Makes about 8 cups (64 fl oz / 2 l)

1 fresh parsley stem
1 bay leaf
1 fresh thyme sprig
3 lb (1.5 kg) turkey or chicken necks and backs
2 celery stalks
2 carrots, peeled
2 small yellow onions, root ends trimmed but peel intact, cut into halves
1 leek, including tender green tops, carefully washed and sliced
salt

1. To make a bouquet garni, place the parsley stem, bay leaf and thyme sprig on a small square of cheesecloth (muslin), bring the corners together and tie securely with string.

2. In a 4-qt (4-l) stockpot, combine the poultry pieces, celery, carrots, onions, leek and bouquet garni. Add enough cold water to the stockpot to cover the ingredients. Place over medium heat, uncovered, and bring slowly to a boil.

3. Reduce the heat as low as possible and simmer, uncovered, for 2½–3 hours. Add salt to taste. Stir to mix well.

4. Line a large sieve or a colander with cheesecloth (muslin) and strain the stock through it into a large bowl. Let cool, cover and refrigerate until a layer of fat solidifies on top. Using a large spoon, lift or spoon off the hardened fat and discard it. If not using immediately, pour the stock into tightly covered containers and refrigerate for up to 3 days or freeze for up to 2 months.

Per 1 Cup Serving: Calories 30 (Kilojoules 127), Protein 2 g, Carbohydrates 3 g, Total Fat 1 g, Saturated Fat 0 g, Cholesterol 0 mg, Sodium 47 mg, Dietary Fiber 0 g

INDEX